Wood Knocks
Journal of Sasquatch Research

Wood Knocks
Journal of Sasquatch Research

by David Weatherly

Leprechaun Press
ARIZONA • 2016

Wood Knocks
Journal of Sasquatch Research
by David Weatherly

ISBN: 978-0-6927-1034-0 (Paperback)

Published by:

Leprechaun Press
Arizona

Cover by: Sam Shearon
www.mister-sam.com

Edited by: A. Dale Triplett
www.daletriplett.com

Interior design by: SMAK
www.smakgraphics.com

Printed in the United States of America

Table of Contents

List of Illustrations and Maps

Image	**Page #**

List of Contributors, Photo Credits

Editor's Preface

Cryptids and credibility are seldom reconcilable in this era of sensationalism, hoax-driven journalism and for-profit publications that accomplish little to nothing but insult cogent research and the diligent, hard-working seekers of truth. David Weatherly has brought together an amazing group that slaps the charlatans right up side the head, and this debut volume of Wood Knocks is a welcome breath of fresh, truth-seeking air.

The contributors for this edition are not armchair enthusiasts rehashing readily available material from the web. Far from it. Just trust the guy that had to try and pin down these globe-trotting researchers for edits, images and clarification. Some days I thought it would be easier on me just to simply walk in the woods and interview Bigfoot myself! These researchers spend far more time in the woods and wilds than they ever do in front of a computer, and this anthology reflects just a tiny glimpse into their tireless dedication to lending much-needed credence to cryptozoology.

This work represents some of the best and brightest this field has to offer, and I welcome you on this global foray into substance, curiosity and the delightful wonder of the elusive Sasquatch.

-A. Dale Triplett

Author's Introduction

Back in 1967, a pair of cowboys in Northern California captured a now legendary piece of movie footage. Known as the Patterson-Gimlin film, (after the two men, Roger Patterson and Bob Gimlin) the brief clip shows a large, hairy creature moving quickly over the terrain and away from the two men and their horses.

Without a doubt, the clip is one of the most examined pieces of film footage in history. Even today, there's still much debate about the authenticity of the film, but one thing is certain, it helped inspire generations of cryptozoologists in their quest to find Bigfoot.

Of course, reports of these creatures predate the film and come from all corners of the globe. America, Australia, China, Russia, the list goes on and on, and each region has its own name for the beast. Yeti, Yowie, Sasquatch, and, perhaps the most familiar to those in the west, Bigfoot.

Fast forward almost fifty years after the famous film and the topic of Sasquatch is hotter than ever. Reality television shows, books, magazines, feature films, the creature seems to be everywhere, even though it hasn't officially been found.

Now, adding to the mix, I'm proud to present the first volume of "Wood Knocks: A Journal of Sasquatch Research."

I've recruited some of the best researchers and writers in the field of cryptozoology and let them have their say about various aspects of the creature known as Bigfoot.

If the stunning cover by artist Sam Shearon wasn't enough to make you pick up this volume, then the contents should seal the deal.

A fantastic piece by Lyle Blackburn exploring the giants of the piney woods kicks things off and the volume doesn't slow down from there.

Linda Godfrey, known for her copious research into dogman sightings weighs in with a piece on Bigfoot in southern Wisconsin.

From across the pond two Richards have made great contributions. Richard Freeman with details on the orang-pendak, Sumatra's "short man," and Richard Muirhead who looks at Hong Kong as a focal point for Bigfoot and Yeren studies.

My own contribution in this volume covers encounters with the hairy man on native land deep in the southwest of the United States.

And there's still more. Prolific writer Nick Redfern address the sound of Sasquatch, scholar Micah Hanks delves into the folklore of abductions by Bigfoot and the always fascinating Ken Gerhard ask the question, "Is Bigfoot a giant form of homo erectus?"

So dive in, there's plenty of fascinating information awaiting on the creature that we hear so much of, yet know so little about.

-David Weatherly

Giants of the Piney Woods

by Lyle Blackburn

At an early age I was fascinated by Bigfoot. It was a fascination that filled my young mind with wonder, but also trepidation. While I was thoroughly enamored with the mystery, I remember a twinge of fear when I first saw the alleged creature stroll across Bluff Creek in televised airings of the Patterson-Gimlin film. Could a huge, hairy man-ape like the one shown in the grainy footage really be living in the forests of North America? It was a question that loomed like a shadow over my youth.

At the time I was already familiar with woodland settings not unlike Bluff Creek, having been a part of my dad's hunting obsession. Every weekend during deer season I found myself camped out at my father's lease near Possum Kingdom, Texas, enjoying campfires and enduring long, silent hours in tree stands. During those times, I would sit back and listen to the sounds of the woods; the insects, the birds, the coyotes yipping at sundown, and oftentimes a lonely oil derrick pumping steadily in the distance. It was relaxing, but also challenging to remain still while sitting atop a few uncomfortable two-by-fours nailed into the crook of a tree. (This qualified as a tree stand back in those days.)

On occasion, the subject of Bigfoot would creep into my thoughts as we sat there waiting for a deer, but it was only in terms of the mystery, not fear. After all, what would I have to worry about? Bigfoot lived in the faraway mountains of the Pacific Northwest, not in Texas. I had a much better chance of seeing a 30-point trophy buck than a Bigfoot... or did I?

My father's side of the family is from a small East Texas town called Carthage. The quaint community is located near the Louisiana border within the thickly forested area of the state known as the East Texas Pine Belt, or more commonly, the Piney Woods. Every spring we made a three-hour pilgrimage from our home near Fort Worth to Carthage for a family reunion centered around my great-grandmother's birthday. (A tradition that would continue until her death at the age of 106!)

As we departed each year, I would begrudge the lackluster scenery as we made our way east of Dallas. The area is known as the Blackland Prairie and thus made up of tall-grass prairies bordered by patchy wooded areas mostly consisting of mesquite, hackberry, and elm. It did not provide much visual stimulation for a boy my age, so I would resolve to read comic books or pester my sister until my dad threatened to stop the car.

But my childish impatience would always subside as we approached the Piney Woods. There my focus was drawn outside the car, as oak groves and grass began to give way to loblolly and longleaf pines, crowding like green goliaths on either side of the roadway. It was like leaving the canvas of a cowboy portrait for a place where sky-scraping trees ruled the landscape. We were still in Texas, but it was not the Texas I was used to, not even that of our hunting lease in Central Texas. Possum Kingdom had its share of woodlands, of course, but it's part of the Rolling Plains region where broad savannas and scattered trees reflect the more stereo-typical Texas backdrop. Traveling east into the Piney Woods was something altogether different.

As we rolled further into the thickening evergreens I would stare into the shadowy recesses, imagining what strange animals or interesting people might live within. There was something about the canopy of those great pines that beckoned to me, much like the mystery of Bigfoot. But it would be years before I made the connection between that area and the hairy hominid that haunted my thoughts. It was only when I began to delve deeper and more seriously into the Bigfoot phenomenon I realized my chances of seeing a Bigfoot in Texas, perhaps in those very woods, were greater than I had ever imagined. The legend of Bigfoot did exist beyond the confines of the Pacific Northwest, and was likely walking on two legs through the vast thickets of East Texas.

****

In 1986, near the Sabine River in Panola County not far from my great-grandmother's home, Jeff Stewart was camping with friends as they often did on weekends (fig. 1-1). He was 15 at the time and already a skilled outdoorsman, having grown up in a culture of hunting and fishing typical of that area. The spot where they camped was located on 580 heavily wooded acres owned by his family, of which he was intimately familiar both in terms of geography and wildlife… or so he thought.

Earlier in the day he and his friends caught a load of catfish in the river and cleaned them at an old pump-well present on the property. Afterwards, they intentionally threw the entrails on the ground so they could return at night with flashlights to harvest any fur-bearing animals caught eating the scraps. Stewart had done this plenty of times in the past with successful results.

Later that night, after eating their fill of fish, Stewart was volunteered to go check the trap. Chiding his friends for being lazy, he grabbed his flashlight and .22 rifle and headed off down the trail. As he approached the spot, he could see something there eating, dimly lit in the beam of his old two-cell bulb. It was rather large and hairy, so he assumed it was a hog. However, when Stewart got within 20 yards, the thing stood up on two legs.

Fig. 1-1: Sabine River Area
(photo by Lyle Blackburn)

3

"I never will forget," Stewart told me during one of several conversations we've had about the event, "It never made a gesture; it just looked me dead in the face."

His first thought was that someone must be playing a joke on him, perhaps one of his friends. He even called out to it, indicating he wasn't falling for the ruse. But the more he looked at the silent figure standing before him, the more he realized it was not a person in a costume, if it was even a person at all. He had heard stories about people living down in the river bottoms that had gone feral; people who had gone down there to live and were rarely seen again. But this looked more like an animal. It was beastly despite its anthropomorphic stature.

He described it as being approximately five feet tall and covered in hair matted down with a layer of gray, gumbo mud from the river bottom. The face was exposed, with very dark, oily and weathered skin that reminded him of an Australian Aborigine. It had dark eyes and a nose that was wide and almost ape-like, but still within human parameters.

Unsure of what the creature might do, Stewart leveled his gun at it. But he didn't have to pull the trigger. Seconds later the creature took three steps backward in a distinct "toe to heel" fashion.

"When it got to the edge of the bushes, where there was a pine thicket, it was still looking at me and it just kind of disappeared backwards into the brush," Stewart told me.

After it was out of sight, the stunned teenager ran back to camp where he told his friends about the encounter. Stewart was outwardly shaken, but still they dismissed his story with a laugh, thinking perhaps he was trying to scare them. Realizing it would be hard to convince *anyone* he'd truly seen such a thing, he resolved to stay quiet for many years. Other reports of a hairy, Bigfoot-like creature in the area – often referred to as the "Sabine Thing" – added credence to Stewart's claim, but at the time he was alone in his experience.

If residents of East Texas are dubious about Bigfoot sightings in their own backwoods, then certainly those who have not traversed the diverse eco-regions of Texas will find it hard to imagine any such creature could exist in a state more associated with cowboys than hairy giants. But the fact is Texas contains an abundance of forestry and rain-rich conditions necessary to support – and obscure, if necessary –

an array of wildlife. According to a 2011 Forest Inventory and Analysis report by the Texas Forest Service, there are 62.4 million acres of forests and woodlands in Texas which cover nearly 38 percent of the state's massive land area. The East Texas Pine Belt (Piney Woods) is the principal forest region, consisting of 43 counties extending from Bowie and Red River counties in northeast Texas, to Jefferson, Harris, and Waller counties in southeast Texas. The counties contain 12.1 million acres of forestland, of which 11.9 million acres are classified as productive timberland (fig. 1-2). Within and beyond this region there are numerous lakes, ponds, rivers, swamps and other waterways that stand in stark contrast to the dusty ranch scenery that popularize Texas stereotypes. Brush country landscapes are certainly present in other parts of the state, but don't carry the extensive history of man-ape sightings as the eastern forests do.

1. Piney Woods
2. Blackland Prairies
3. Coastal Sand Plains
4. Edwards Plateau
5. Gulf Coast Prairies & Marshes
6. High Plains
7. Llano Uplift
8. Oak Woods & Prairies
9. Rolling Plains
10. South Texas Brush Country
11. Trans Pecos

Fig. 1-2: Natural Regions of Texas

Sightings, like the one reported by Stewart can be traced back many years in the area. In the winter of 1969, Teresa Dixon, her aunt, and her little sister (all very young at the time) were exploring a patch of fire-damaged woods behind their grandmother's house near Beckville in Panola County. They had just crossed a field and entered the wood line when they noticed some kind of animal crouching behind the trees. As soon as they made eye contact, it stood up... on two legs.

"It was very tall, thin, and hairy like an ape, but was more man-like," Dixon told me when I followed up on the report. She's unsure of the exact distance they were from the creature, but she distinctly remembers seeing its eyes. "It didn't look menacing," she recalled. "And it wasn't scared."

But the girls were scared. So much so they turned and ran as fast as they could back to their grandmother's house, which sat beyond a large field and a barbed wire fence . "I don't remember how I got over that fence," Dixon said. "But I'll never forget what I saw that day. It's tattooed on my brain."

After telling her family of the experience, her grandfather admitted that he had seen an ape-like creature several years before near their house. As a man of few words, he kept it quiet so as not to frighten anyone.

Approximately two years after Dixon's sighting, around 1971, her uncle claimed to have seen a similar creature while camping in the bottoms between Beckville and Carthage. Locals in that area – often referred to as "the river bottoms" though no river ran through it – also told of a strange beast allegedly responsible for many unexplained livestock deaths. The sightings are secondhand and unsubstantiated, but given the credible testimony by Ms. Dixon, it's hard to completely dismiss the possibility that a strange animal was living there (just miles from my great-grandmother's house!).

Another sighting in Panola County was reported by Paul Matlock. After first hearing of his experience through fellow colleagues – who interviewed Matlock and judged his story credible – I was able to speak to him myself. What follows is one of the most bone-chilling Bigfoot encounters I've ever heard.

According to Matlock, he was hog hunting in March 2003 on a strip of land tucked away on the Texas-side of the Sabine River. As the sun began to rise, he could hear a group of hogs snorting and rooting as they made their way toward a pile of apple and potato slices he had thrown out about 20 yards from his tree stand.

While waiting for a clear shot, Matlock caught a glimpse of something moving between the trees 30 yards to the right of the hogs. He raised his rifle to get a better look through his 3x9 scope. At first he could only see the side of a dark face peering out from behind a leafless tree, but after a few moments the thing stood up and moved to another tree. Now the hunter could see it was some sort of huge, hairy creature able to walk on two legs. It didn't look like any animal he'd seen before, and it didn't appear to be another hunter... even one in a ghillie suit. In fact, it didn't look like a person at all.

Despite a growing sense of alarm, Matlock turned the scope up to maximum power and trained it on the animal as it worked from one tree to another. Each time, the creature would crouch down on all fours and leap to the next tree where it would land at the base and stand up. It would then study the hogs intently before moving again. Its every movement was fluid and completely silent.

Matlock described it as being six to seven feet tall with a thick coat of reddish-brown hair covering most of its body except for the hands, feet, and part of the face. The face itself looked human-like with dark brown eyes and small ears. The body was very heavily built and had breasts. Apparently it was a female.

The stalking continued for several more minutes until the hogs - five total - were less than 30 yards from Matlock. Then all at once the thing crouched on all fours, curled its knuckles, and leapt towards its prey. As soon as it hit the ground it let out a blood-curdling scream that pierced the morning air. The hogs instantly panicked and scattered, but it was too late. Within two leaps the creature had descended upon them, slapping one hog so hard on its side that it flew through the air and slammed into a nearby tree. When the squealing pig hit the ground, the creature leapt on it, first grabbing its neck with the right hand and then pummeling it with the huge fist of its left. "I could hear ribs cracking with every hit," Matlock told me.

The remaining four hogs bolted into the woods. By the time their squeals faded, their sibling lay dead at the hands of the creature who then scooped it up under one arm as if it were no more than a pillow sack. The thing let out a series of whooping sounds which were immediately answered by shorter whoops from an unseen animal deeper in the woods.

Matlock felt a sense of relief when the creature began to walk off, but it was short-lived. Without warning the creature dropped the hog to the ground and turned its head in the direction of his tree stand. At first it looked past the hunter with its eyes scanning at ground level, but then tilted its head upwards and followed the tree trunk until its eyes focused on him. The beast studied Matlock intently for a few moments, moving its head slightly as it did, while at the same time opening its mouth to reveal a set of yellowed teeth Then suddenly, as if it were satisfied, the creature bent down to retrieve the hog, tucked it under its arm, and casually walked off into the trees.

Matlock watched through his trembling scope until he could no longer see the thing. After he was sure it was gone, he lowered his gun and sat there for approximately 30 minutes trying to calm himself down. In the end, he decided if the creature wanted to hurt him it could have. So he crawled down from the tree stand and quickly made his way out of the woods.

Upon listening to the details and questioning him at length, I could find no justifiable reason to dismiss his testimony. It was something that seemed to have had a profound effect on him.

"Let's put it this way," Matlock told me. "I will never go in the woods again without feeling on edge. It's not something you forget."

Fig 1-3: East Texas Counties

****

While the creature in Matlock's story acted in an alarming and aggressive manner, its actions were directed at an animal, presumably to secure a meal. However, there are other cases where the alleged Bigfoots turned on humans. According to an article in the *Marshall News Messenger* dated September 1, 1965, 13-year-old Johnny Maples was walking along a rural road in nearby Marion County on the afternoon of August 20 when he heard a noise in the bushes (fig. 1-3). He thought it might be a friend who lived nearby, so he called out. When the "person" did not answer, he threw a few rocks into the bushes figuring it was just a small animal. Suddenly, a "large hairy man or beast" emerged from the trees behind a fence, presumably having been hit by one of the rocks. Maples panicked and started running down the road.

9

According to the boy, the beast immediately jumped the fence and started after him. "I ran as hard and fast as I could, but he kept up with me and he wasn't running, either, just sort of walking along behind me," Maples told the reporter. Maples even ditched his shoes in order to run faster, all the while looking back to see the hairy beast in pursuit. "The last time I turned around the beast had gone off the road and disappeared into the woods. I could hear him moving around but I didn't see him again," Maples stated.

The teenager was eventually picked up farther down the road by a neighbor in a car and taken home where he told the story to his mother, who noted her son was in a "state of shock." The Marion County Deputy Sheriff was called to the scene but could find no evidence, tracks or otherwise.

Maples described the beast as a seven-foot-tall ape with long black hair all over its body except for the face, stomach, and palms of its hands which, he noted, "hung down below his knees." His claim of such an alarming creature apparently set off a monster hunt. In a UPI article titled "Town Fed Up With Monster Hunters" (September 20, 1965), Sheriff Luke Walker of Jefferson, Texas, told a reporter that Bigfoot hunters from three states had overrun his small town since the news of Maples' encounter had spread.

A particularly harrowing report of murderous, ape-like creatures around the same time was recorded by the now defunct *Bigfoot Bulletin* (Issue #22, October 31, 1970). The report was submitted by Nick E. Campbell, an Army trainee stationed at Fort Ord, California. Campbell relates that two of his fellow trainees from the Texas National Guard, Private David Lawson and Private Royal Jacobs, both from Longview, Texas (on the eastern reaches of the Piney Woods), told him that: "In or about the year 1965, there was a rash of reports of a giant hairy creature roaming the thickets and back country between Jefferson and Longview, Texas, but nearest to Longview. A man and his little daughter reported it as being large, black and not a bear. Several head of cattle and a couple of people were supposedly killed by it. Private Jacobs was a member of a posse that hunted the creature when he was a teenager. He told me that he saw the body of one of the murdered persons and that the victim had been torn apart. At the time he threw his gun back in the car and went home."

Jacobs, Campbell said, was a licensed minister and he would

vouch for the truthfulness of both men. There must have been some preceding reports or information since the section is titled "Concerning the Longview, Texas, Reports." But as it stands, this is the only written information available regarding these rather outrageous claims. According to Craig Woolheater, founder of the Texas Bigfoot Research Center, an investigation into the matter was conducted by Bigfoot researcher Charles DeVore. The trail led to Dwain Dennis, a journalist and Jefferson resident who actually interviewed Johnny Maples at the time he claimed to have been chased by the "monster." Dennis had also looked into the 1965 killings reported in the Bigfoot Bulletin but found no evidence that a posse was formed to hunt the creatures down, or that there were ever any killings in Marion County that could be blamed on Bigfoot.

In 1979, a family's serene Easter Sunday turned into a nightmare when they allegedly encountered an aggressive, ape-like creature several miles south of Jefferson in Harrison County. According to a report filed in 2000 with the Texas Bigfoot Research Center (now the North American Wood Ape Conservancy), a couple and their two young girls were enjoying the afternoon on a 460 acre tract of property near Woodlawn when they heard a "loud crunching" in the brush. They could not see an animal but were spooked enough to return to their car. At that point, the husband decided to do some target shooting with his pistol near a deep ravine. According to the woman: "We shot several times when suddenly, a large animal lunged into the ravine in front of us only about 10 to 15 feet. He paused, looked at us and then in one leap, jumped out of [the] ravine. We froze for a moment then [my] husband grabbed our six year old and I took the hand of the nine year old. We ran towards the car."

They could hear the animal pursuing them as it crashed through the surrounding brush, but apparently stopped before it reached the car. She described the animal as being grayish in color, covered in five to six inch long hair, under which they could still see skin. It had wide shoulders, long arms, and was "powerful looking." She added, "Unlike the drawings of Bigfoot, he had a short neck and round head. Far more human looking than the blocky thick shapes of the drawings."

The frightened family promptly fled the scene in their car.

Another startling, up-close encounter occurred in the same vicinity in 1989. The experience was recounted to me by Brad

11

McAndrews, a person with whom I've been acquainted for several years. At the time, he was visiting his grandmother's cabin, located in the thick woods surrounding Jefferson. One afternoon while he was scouting along an old path, McAndrews heard something large moving through the woods. Thinking he might get a glimpse of a deer, he waited anxiously as the crack of pine saplings and the crunching of leaves grew louder. Finally, an animal did emerge from the brush, but it was definitely not a deer. It was an ape-like creature approximately seven to eight feet tall with dark, reddish-brown hair and weathered looking skin. At first it was running on all fours, but upon seeing McAndrews, it stopped and rose up on two legs. In his own words:

"At about 15-20 yards to my right, it came into view and turned to its right. It was moving, on all fours, at what I would call a hustled pace, almost as if it was running from something. When it was at about 9-12 yards from me and about two feet off of the roadway, it used a rather large wooden fence post to hoist itself into a bipedal progression, using its left arm and hand. Its change in gait or posture did not result in a change in its speed. It then took a few running steps before passing behind a five foot sapling and stopping right before me. When it reached me, it immediately stopped and squared its shoulders at me. I had never been so scared in my life."

McAndrews held his breath as he stood transfixed on the creature. For several seconds it alternated between looking at him and looking away, as if it were unsure of what to do next. Upon hearing McAndrew's brother shout from a distance, the animal suddenly sprinted off on two legs, using its hands to tunnel its way through the thick trees. Relieved, Brad turned and ran toward his brother as fast as his legs could carry him. It was an experience that haunts him to this day.

Just east of Jefferson lies the beautifully scenic Caddo Lake, one of the Piney Woods' most impressive landmarks (fig. 1-4). Caddo is the largest natural freshwater lake in the South, encompassing upwards of 35,000 acres as it spans across the border of Texas into the bayou lands of Louisiana. The lake is a naturalist's dream of serene waters and majestic woodlands, but also a place that can evoke shivers as the sun goes down behind the moss-draped cypress trees. Among these woods, locals claim, lurks a Bigfoot creature known as the Caddo Critter.

Sightings of the Caddo Critter may have a history predating European settlers. According to my colleague Kathy Strain, archaeologist and author of *Giants, Cannibals & Monsters: Bigfoot in Native Culture,* the Caddo Indian tribes that first populated the area used the word *Ha'yacatsi* to describe a race of "lost giants" said to live there. When this word is considered in terms of the Giants of the Piney Woods, then no doubt it could apply to the creature we call Bigfoot.

In modern times, sightings of these "Texas Bigfoot" are so notable in the vicinity of Caddo Lake, that the town of Jefferson has declared one Saturday in October as "Bigfoot Day." The corresponding weekend typically hosts a long-running Bigfoot Conference which attracts numerous enthusiasts. Caddo Lake has also been used as the location for several Bigfoot-themed movies including *Creature From Black Lake (1976), Boggy Creek: The Legend is True (2010), and Skookum: The Hunt for Bigfoot (2014).*

Fig 1-4: Caddo Lake
(photo by Lyle Blackburn)

****

In the woodlands north of Jefferson, more reports of the Texas Bigfoot have been documented over the years. In October 1984, a witness claimed to have seen a startling creature in Bowie County located in the far northeast corner of the state. In a report filed in 2005 with the Texas Bigfoot Research Center, the witness said she was walking along Anderson Creek (a tributary of the Sulphur River) one evening around dusk when she began to hear the sound of footsteps in the leaves as a rank smell entered her nostrils. Looking towards the sound, she was confronted by the sight of something standing by the edge of the water. It had rained earlier in the day, leaving a light fog hanging in the air, but still enough visibility to see it was not human.

The thing, she recalled, was approximately seven feet tall with a body covered in black hair. It had long arms that hung down almost to its knees. In the foggy dusk it was hard to make out facial details, but she was certain it had no visible ears atop its head which would indicate a bear. Frightened, the witness turned and ran as fast as she could back home, never looking back to see if the creature was following.

"I have never been as scared as I was in that moment," the witness reported. "I remember seeing it breathe. It was completely motionless except for the slight movement as it breathed in and out, and that is what frightened me so very bad, because I knew that it was real and I was not just seeing something among the trees."

Perhaps something unknown had been living in the Anderson Creek bottoms for years. According to local rumors, a farmer allegedly found strange tracks near his well in the 1940s.

More recently, I was contacted by Jami Longacre, who lives in Cass County just south of Bowie. She and her husband live in the countryside of Atlanta, Texas, where they've experienced a string of alarming incidents.

The first occurred in July 2012. That night the couple were entertaining friends in their backyard when they heard an eerie, scream-like roar coming from the woods at around 10:30 p.m. Alarmed, the Longacres and their friends listened, but did not hear it again.

Later, around midnight, they were preparing for bed when they heard three booming whoops outside the house. The noise was so loud, it sounded as if the animal – or whatever had made the sound – was standing right outside their bedroom window. "It scared us so bad, the hair on the back of our necks actually stood up," she told me.

After a few moments without any further sounds, Jami's husband went to the front door, slowly opened it and looked out. He did not see anything out of the ordinary, but could smell a pungent odor, as if an animal had been there moments before. He quickly closed and locked the door.

A short time later, the couple relaxed enough to venture outside to have a better look around. Again, they did not see anything strange, but did hear another screaming whoop deeper in the woods to the west. It made them feel better knowing the thing had apparently moved on, but they were still on edge.

By February 2013, Jami had all but forgotten the spooky incidents as she and a co-worker drove home from their night-shift job. As Jami slowed to turn onto her county road, she glanced over to see a tall animal standing in the ditch beside the road. The ditch was at least five feet deep, yet she could still see part of its huge mass above the ditch line, touching the low-hanging branches of the tree above it. It looked to be reddish-brown in color.

Her friend saw the startled look on her face and asked what was the matter. Before she could reply, the figure ran behind the car and disappeared into the blackness. She couldn't make out details of its shape in her rearview mirror, but she was sure it ran behind them because it flashed across the reflectors mounted on the neighbor's mailbox.

"I don't know if it was Bigfoot, but I know it was huge and the color of dead pine straw," she said. "And it scared me to death."

To the west of Cass County, more reported Bigfoot sightings can be found. According to an article in the July 1979 issue of *Fate* magazine, one incident dates back to 1969, when two men said they encountered a strange creature near a levee which runs parallel to the South Sulphur River, about 10 miles from Commerce, Texas, in Hunt County. Kenneth Wilson was first in the area around 11:00 p.m. hanging out with three friends. As he sat in his car, his friends (one man and two women) were out walking along the levee. Wilson heard something moving in the bushes around him, then a short time later heard his friends start screaming. They rushed back to the car in a panic, saying they had seen something down by the levee.

Frightened, Wilson drove the group to a nearby gas station where their friend Jerry Matlock worked. They asked to borrow his gun.

Not wanting to part with the gun, Matlock accompanied them back to the area to investigate. When they arrived, they were greeted with a shocking sight as a huge, man-like creature covered in brown hair jumped over the levee and ran towards the car. "This thing was bigger than any man I've ever seen in my life," Matlock told the reporter. "You could have stretched a [3-foot] yardstick across its shoulders and its shoulders would've been wider than that."

Wilson also got a glimpse of the creature, saying "It was big and hairy, whatever it was." At that point he hit the gas and spun the car around. As they sped off, the man in the front passenger seat tried to fire at the beast with Matlock's gun, but the gun did not go off.

The next day Wilson and Matlock returned to the scene where they found foot-prints. "I put my arm down in one of the prints," Matlock said, "and that print was as long as from my elbow to the tip of my outstretched fingers."

Another sighting in proximity of the South Sulphur River occurred in August 1978 (fig. 1-5). As documented in the same Fate article, High School Senior, Harvey Garrison, was driving along a country road at about 10:15 p.m. when he claimed to have seen a seven-foot-tall creature standing by the side of the road.

"I slammed on my brakes and came within a few feet of hitting the thing," he told investigators. "It turned slightly toward my car. Then in one step it was across the road!" It disappeared into the blackness of the night.

Two days later, three more teenagers from the small community of South Sulphur west of Commerce were reportedly frightened by a similar beast while walking on the very same road at midnight. Upon hearing something moving in the trees, they walked over to investigate when a large animal jumped up and ran away. They described it as being larger than a gorilla.

Fig. 1-5: Sulphur River
(photo by Lyle Blackburn)

These sightings in Hunt County are outside the area classified as the East Texas Pine Belt, yet it's not an unlikely location. Not only is the area around Commerce sufficiently wooded, but flanked on either side by the Middle and South Sulphur Rivers. These bodies of water eventually converge and flow eastward into Wright Patman Lake, and exit Texas near the town of Fouke, Arkansas, home of the famous Legend of Boggy Creek.

For those that have read my book, *The Beast of Boggy Creek: The True Story of the Fouke Monster,* then the significance of the Sulphur River is obvious. If you haven't read my book (yet), then suffice to say numerous sightings of the legendary creature made famous by the 1972 movie, *The Legend of Boggy Creek*, occurred along its banks and in the swampy bottomlands surrounding it. Given this, it would not be out of the question for such creatures to travel up and down the river way searching for food or higher ground during times of flooding. The banks of the Sulphur River all throughout its expanse are concealed with lush greenery and thick woods.

I recently documented a very convincing sighting near the Sulphur River, positioned within the borders of Texas, yet not far from Fouke. The woman (who asked to remain anonymous) said she was driving north from her home at around 10:00 a.m. on November 24, 2014, when she realized she had forgotten something. As she completed a three-point turn on the narrow county thoroughfare and began to head back south, she was startled by something standing in the middle of the road. At first she thought it was a kid dressed in a Halloween costume, but as she focused on the figure, she realized it was some sort of hairy animal, one that walked on two legs.

The creature had apparently come out of the thick patch of woods on her left and was crossing the road where her car had been moments before. Now that she had turned around, it paused as if caught in the act. The creature stood fully upright with an estimated height of five feet[1]. It was covered in reddish-brown hair, except for the face which had dark, leathery skin and particularly piercing eyes. She could see the wispy hair on its arms waving in the gentle morning breeze. It gazed at the woman for a few seconds before turning and running back into the woods.

As she recounted the story in person to myself and my research partner, Tom Shirley, we could hear the emotion in her voice. We watched the earnest expression in her eyes. It was apparent that feelings of fear and bewilderment still lingered. "It scared me to death," she told us.

I asked her if there was any possibility it could have been a person in a costume, perhaps trying to scare passersby? "At first I thought it was a kid in a costume, but the more I looked at it, I could see it wasn't," she explained. "When it was running, it didn't look like a costume, it looked like a real animal."

Tom and I visited the location where she said the creature entered the road (fig. 1-6). The thick woods standing to the east were indeed a likely place for an animal to emerge. There were a few houses in the

---

1   The woman was puzzled that the figure's apparent height of five feet did not equal the towering Bigfoot stature she had heard about, so I explained it's only logical that if these creatures are real, then naturally there would be younger ones that have not reached full maturity, not to mention I had heard plenty of other witness reports where the creatures were of varying heights from four to eight feet. Her description was not out of the ordinary, and in fact, quite common in the attributes of its reddish-brown hair and darker facial skin.

vicinity, but it was a very rural setting with the houses far apart and mostly nestled into the trees. A large, open field sat on the opposite side of the road, presumably where the creature was headed. I wasn't sure why it would want to cross into such an open area, but regardless, if a large animal were to move around there, this seemed like the mostly like place.

***Fig. 1-6: Location where the woman said she
saw the creature in the road.***
(photo by Lyle Blackburn)

As Tom and I took a few photos and poked around in the woods just off the road, inevitably a resident drove up and questioned our intentions. The person was initially suspicious but after I explained who I was, it led to a phone conversation with the person who owned the wooded property. When I told him a woman had claimed to see a Bigfoot-like creature cross the road there, he was intrigued. He wasn't aware of any other reports or tales from his neighbors, but did tell me that aside from a few houses, the woods basically ran unimpeded for miles in the direction of Fouke.

I also asked him if it was possible some kids in the area had dressed up in a Bigfoot costume in the days preceding Thanksgiving. He told me there were no kids other than his own that lived along that stretch of road, and that it was highly unlikely. He also pointed out kids would have been in school the morning of Monday, November 24.

Considering all the information, it seemed as though the woman had a legitimate encounter which is not only significant in regards to its probability, but its proximity to the Sulphur River. The river passes just south of the road where she claimed to have seen the creature. In fact, if you were to keep driving, you would find yourself floating in the Sulphur since the road literally dead-ends into its muddy waters.

****

The proximity to water in many of these Southern Bigfoot cases is an interesting aspect, and one that may lend credence to witness testimony. Early Bigfoot researchers/authors such as John Green *(Sasquatch: The Apes Among Us)* and Loren Coleman *(Bigfoot! The True Story of Apes in America)* noticed right away that most Bigfoot sightings in the Deep South – whether in Texas or other states – occurred near rivers, lakes, or swamplands. *The Legend of Boggy Creek* is a prime example, where sightings of the Fouke Monster were prominent along Boggy Creek, the Sulphur River, or within Mercer Bayou. In Texas we have already noted sightings along the Sabine River, Sulphur Rivers, Anderson Creek, and Caddo Lake, and will continue to see this theme as we examine more sightings.

The significance of water is one that cannot be overlooked for several reasons. First, if large creatures such as Bigfoot were to exist in the southlands, they would need plenty of water to offset the high heat conditions that prevail much of the year. Without a copious water supply, the creatures simply could not survive. Water not only provides hydration but ensures the proliferation of vegetation and animal-life critical to the diet of an incredibly large animal.

Waterways also function as "wildlife highways." With the ever-encroaching development imposed by humans, the areas of rivers, creeks, bogs, and bayous tend to remain untouched, thus providing an environment where animals can live and travel in relative peace. Bigfoot would absolutely depend on places like this in order to move around.

And finally, water – specifically rainwater – is necessary to grow thick woodlands which would be critical to hiding such a conspicuous resident as Bigfoot. Not surprisingly, East Texas has the highest percentage of annual rainfall in the state, ranging from 40 up to 50 inches per year at the eastern tip. This not only corresponds to the location of the Piney Woods, but also to the majority of Bigfoot sightings, which primarily occur where the annual rainfall exceeds 40 inches per year. This is not to say there aren't other credible reports that have occurred in other places outside this zone, but even in those cases they almost always correspond to a nearby body of water.

So it is either coincidence that people who "make up" stories about seeing huge, bipedal apes in Texas most often choose a setting near water or high annual rainfall, or the proximity of water sparks outrageous misidentifications and hallucinations. Or perhaps, the particular locations of the reported sightings provide circumstantial support to the theory that proposes if Bigfoots do exist in the South, they would naturally be seen near this sort of habitat more often than not.

One of the most significant waterways in Texas is the Red River which flows along the state's northern border. It's the second-largest river basin in the southern Great Plains, extending across several ecoregions of the state, including the Piney Woods, as it moves into southwest Arkansas and on into Louisiana, where it eventually merges with the Mississippi.

As expected, the Red River area has a history of sightings that tie into the premise of Bigfoot creatures inhabiting the Piney Woods and nearby waterways. A 1965 article from *The Paris News* documents sightings of a strange creature in northwest Lamar County near the town of Direct. Obviously written in response to Associated Press circulation of the Marion County "Caddo Critter" incidents from September that same year, the article states that: "Residents in and around Direct say they know just how the folks around Caddo, Tex., feel when their 'critter' jumps from the bushes."

According to the article, a woman claimed to have seen a creature referred to by locals as the "Manimal." She was out one evening near her house when she spotted the thing with her flashlight. Frightened, she hurried back to the house where she and her cousin watched it jump a fence on all fours, then stand up on two legs. "It wasn't seven feet tall as the Caddo residents claimed, but about 6-2 as it stood up," she told reporters.[2]

The woman later found tracks at the scene, which were examined by a game warden. Although they are described as being large, they are also said to have claw marks, leaving some doubt as to whether the Manimal even falls into the Bigfoot classification. Either way, the article goes on to say that "oldsters" there claim to have seen the Manimal for more than 50 years.

According to David Holley of the Texoma Bigfoot Research and Investigations Group, old-timers in the area of south Red River County tell of a strange creature or "wildman," near Cuthand Creek during the 1960s and 70s. Referred to as the "Cuthand Critter," it was allegedly seen by farmers and ranchers on several occasions. Holley also heard stories in the 1980s about a "large, hair-covered creature who resembles a huge gorilla" seen walking across some pastures not far from Cuthand Creek.

In April 1982, two boys claim to have seen a Bigfoot-like creature near Bagwell in Red River County. According to a report published by the North American Wood Ape Conservancy, the two boys were sent to fetch their uncle, who was working in a pasture. It was starting to get dark, so the boys hurriedly jumped a fence and started toward their uncle whom they could see in the distance. When they got within fifty feet, however, they came to the stark realization the figure standing there was not their uncle. It was instead a hairy, man-like creature between six and seven feet tall.

"It turned around to look at us, grunted and ran toward the woods," the boys said. "We screamed as it turned."

The animal jumped a fence and disappeared into the dusky twilight, just as their uncle came out of a nearby barn to investigate the commotion. He did not believe their story... until one evening eight months later.

"It was a Saturday night and we were going into town to see a movie. Rain and sleet had been falling most of the day. We lived back off the main road and had to travel logging roads to the highway. About 1,000 yards from our driveway, my aunt suddenly screamed. We looked up in time to see it. It was crossing the road right in front of us. It jumped

---

2   The fact that the woman could make such a precise height estimate makes this report suspicious and should be regarded as such.

across a ditch on the side of the road and disappeared into the woods. In the headlights, the color of the animal was that of a brown bear. He was covered with hair. The hair was not very long. There were missing patches of hair on the arms and legs. Again he seemed to be about six and a half feet tall, kind of sloped up the back."

The boys also said a man who lived near their uncle's house, deeper in the woods, reported seeing a similar creature. "One night he woke up when he heard something rummaging around in the trash barrels out back," the boys said. "He got his shotgun and went outside to shoot what he thought was going to be a raccoon. To his surprise, he was face to face with the creature. He said it grunted and ran away with great speed."

****

At the southern end of the East Texas Pine Belt lies an area known as the Big Thicket. As the bold name suggests, this is a huge, 83,000 acre swath of land full of heavy woods, thick brush, snaking creeks, and blackwater bogs. It's a place of primeval wonder and extreme biological diversity caused by ice age glaciers that pushed the contrasting ecosystems of hardwood forests, prairies, coastal plains, and swamps into one compact area. Outlaws were said to have used it as a hideout, since only the most hardy of lawmen dared to challenge the rugged terrain filled with alligators, snakes, wildcats, and bears. Not surprisingly, the area is also known for a healthy share of strangeness including ghostly lights, lost tribes, wildmen, and of course, Bigfoot.

According to author and Big Thicket expert, Rob Riggs: "For years people in the area between the Thicket's western edge along the Pine Island Bayou and the Trinity River swamp had occasionally caught glimpses of something large, hairy and not quite human." They called it "Ol' Mossyback."

In his book, *In the Big Thicket: On the Trail of the Wild Man*, Riggs recounts an alleged sighting of the creature told to him by a witness. The young man said he was at his home near the Trinity River swamps in Dayton one night when he heard a disturbance outside in his rabbit pens. When he went out to investigate, he saw a "large, dark form" in the moonlight as it fled into the woods with one of his rabbits. The witness impulsively chased the mysterious thief, following squeals of its hapless prey. Upon reaching the river bank a short distance away, he watched "as what looked like a huge ape-like animal swam to the other side of the river, easily negotiating the strong current, and never letting go of the rabbit."

Riggs also obtained witness statements from several young men that claimed multiple sightings of an ape-like creature in the Big Thicket Preserve close to the small town of Saratoga[3]. The boys spent much of their spare time hiking through the Thicket - since there was little else to do - and were therefore very familiar with the local wildlife. This, they assured him, was definitely something out of the ordinary.

The first time they saw it, the creature was running on all fours across a rice field. They were in a truck at a distance of several hundred yards, so very little detail could be observed beyond the fact it looked ape-like. The next time they saw the creature - or one like it - it was creeping around an old bridge at dusk. This time they were much closer and could see it walked in a bipedal fashion. The third encounter occurred near a sludge pit which had been part of an old oil field installation. In this instance they saw what they believed was the same animal right around dusk. As they watched, it let out a long howl before slipping into the woods, never to be seen again.

The multiple encounters seem almost "too lucky," however Riggs heard similar stories from a woman in the area who claimed her family had also seen an ape-like creature on several occasions. On one of those occasions it was seen near a sludge pit. By all accounts the woman and the boys did not know each other.

A more recent sighting was reported by computer systems engineer, James Hendrix. In the fall of 2003, he and his wife, Carrie, were driving near the Big Sandy Creek unit of the Big Thicket National Preserve in Polk County (fig. 1-7). Just after sundown, Hendrix caught sight of something running towards the road through his driver's-side window. He immediately braked as he saw a bipedal figure leap a drainage ditch and run across the road in full view of the headlights. According to Hendrix, it ran fluidly with a bent-over posture, as if it had switched to all-fours once it hit the pavement. He noted that its long arms touched the ground, but only a few times. It was covered in long, reddish-brown hair with an estimated height at around five feet.

"It had a very broad build and looked somewhat like an orangutan

---

3   Saratoga is also notable for its association with Bragg Road, a place famous for a mysterious "ghost light" phenomenon.

except that it had a flat face and was proportioned more like a human with long arms," Hendrix explained. The creature paused when it reached the other side of the road. It looked back at the car before entering the dark woods.

Since the creature assumed a quadrupedal stance, a bear could be considered in this case. However, Hendrix feels strongly it wasn't a bear. "It was running on two legs faster than a person before it went to all fours," he told me on one of the several occasions we discussed the event. His wife also got a good look at the face from approximately 20 feet away as it turned to look at the car. She was sure it did not have the snout of a bear.

An almost identical incident was said to have taken place in November 1972. According to a report filed with the Texas Bigfoot Research Center in 2002, a girl was riding in the car with her grandmother and great aunt one afternoon around 3:30 p.m. when they saw an "ape-like thing" run across the road. They were in a heavily wooded area of Polk County near Big Sandy Creek (which is now part of the Big Thicket National Preserve) driving at a slow speed because the road was unpaved. The girl was leaning forward from the back seat talking to her grandmother and great aunt, when all three saw the creature emerge from the woods on the right and dart across the road. It missed the front bumper by a mere three feet!

They estimated the creature's height at seven to eight feet tall with long arms and long, brown hair that covered its entire body. They didn't recall seeing the face, despite the clear view of its body, since it never turned to look at them in the few seconds it was visible. Like the Hendrix sighting in 2003, the creature ran in a hunched over fashion, swinging its long arms as it went. After it reached the other side of the road, it bounded into the trees never to be seen again.

Fig. 1-7: Big Sandy Creek Area - Big Thicket
(photo by Lyle Blackburn)

****

Another landmark of the Piney Woods is the Sam Houston National Forest. Located several miles southeast of the Big Thicket, the forest is comprised of a massive 163,037 acres, intermingled with privately owned timberland and farms throughout Montgomery, San Jacinto, and Walker counties. Named in honor of the man who ultimately liberated Texas from Mexican rule, Sam Houston Forest not only offers a world of scenic beauty within the heart of Texas, but also the highest concentration of Bigfoot reports in the entire state.

While newspaper accounts from this area are hard to come by, a quick scan of online Bigfoot databases reveals the high number of incident reports for Montgomery, San Jacinto, and Walker. These range from visual sightings to strange noises to footprint discoveries. In one of the oldest Walker County reports posted in the Bigfoot Field Research Organization (BFRO) database, a woman recounts an incident that allegedly happened to her late husband when he was young, around 1960. While he and his friends were hanging out at a cabin near Bedias Creek one night, they sighted a "six-foot-tall-plus being." The boys were familiar with a local legend that said a "hermit" lived in the woods, but the thing they saw didn't seem human— even by woodland hermit standards. According to her husband, it was very large, wore no clothes, and was "totally covered with long dark hair, about 4-6 inches long, all over." He also smelled a rank odor, "somewhat like a moldy skunk."

The woman was interviewed by BFRO investigator, Sybilla Irwin, who deemed her to be credible. As far as the woman could tell, this was a real incident, noting that she could sense the lingering terror whenever her husband spoke of it.

In a report from the neighboring county of San Jacinto, a woman claims to have seen a creature fitting the description of Bigfoot in 1997. According to the North American Wood Ape Conservancy, the woman was driving through the national forest around noon when she noticed something moving in the trees about 70 feet ahead. It appeared to be covered in short, reddish hair, so her first thought was it might be the hindquarters of a horse. However, as she got closer it turned and crouched down, as if trying to hide. As she passed by within 15 to 20 feet, she could see the eyes of the creature following her. She told investigators it looked like "a massive orangutan."

In a report filed with the Gulf Coast Bigfoot Research Organization, a man claimed to have seen a strange creature in the same area years before. According to the report, the man was scouting for deer sign in 1983 when he and his fellow hunters saw an unidentified creature run out of the woods and cross a clearing. "It looked a lot like a monkey, in a way, but it ran on two legs, and never once to my knowledge did it ever use its hands to assist in its motion of travel." He further stated, "It was black in color, approximately 4 [feet] tall, and was really fast."

Famed Canadian Bigfoot researcher John Green also has reports from the area in his extensive files. In a letter dated December 28, 1992, an individual recounted an incident from 1981 in which a woman by the name of Dee Hayes was driving to work through the Sam Houston National Forest at approximately 5:30 a.m. (fig. 1-8). As she rounded a curve in the road, she could see a seven to eight foot tall, brown animal standing on two legs near the side of the road 50 yards away. She stopped and watched the creature until it turned and entered the timber. She described it as having a "gorilla-like" head with no noticeable "snout."

In 2007, an uncanny series of events in Montgomery County further supported the notion that an unknown bipedal entity stalks the woods there. As documented by the North American Wood Ape Conservancy, the first incident occurred on the morning of September

Fig. 1-8: Sam Houston National Forest
(photo by Lyle Blackburn)

19, 2007. At approximately 2:00 a.m., a construction employee working on a new sports facility in The Woodlands was taking a cigarette break when he noticed an upright, bipedal figure step from the woods surrounding the complex. He described it as being exceptionally tall and covered in dark hair. The figure was only visible a few seconds before it slipped back into the trees.

On September 21, two security officers were patrolling the same construction area at 2:20 a.m. when they spotted a huge, bipedal figure walking near the construction office trailers where some makeshift lights had been placed. As they watched the figure from a distance of approximately 30 yards, they could see it stood at least seven feet tall and appeared to be covered in dark hair. It also walked with an unusually long stride, powerful gait, and a slight "slump," all of which did not look human.

After the thing disappeared into the surrounding darkness, the officers reluctantly placed a call to 911, as was their company's policy whenever a trespasser was seen... regardless of its appearance. Police were dispatched - no doubt believing it was probably a human - but no further signs of the trespasser were found. In an interview with NAWAC investigators, the security officer that made the 911 call remained adamant that what he and his partner saw was not a person. He also claimed to have no knowledge of the previous sighting prior to his call.

Five weeks later, a woman reported a similar encounter just one mile from the construction facility. As she and her husband were driving one afternoon, they noticed a "hunched brown figure walking through the trees." As in the other cases, it appeared to be tall, hairy, and human-like. Had the new construction in The Woodlands uprooted an unknown resident? Given the corroborating reports, it's certainly possible (fig. 1-9).

In a final example from this area, researcher and author, Michael Mayes (Texas Cryptid Hunter), along with a friend, saw an unidentified figure in the Walker County section of Sam Houston Forest. On May 14, 2005, the two men were driving along a deserted forest road at 3:15 a.m. when they noticed something standing to their left 30-40 yards ahead. It was the size of a man, but appeared to be covered in a layer of brownish-red hair.

"We had stopped the vehicle on an incline, so only the lower part of the figure was fully illuminated by the headlights," Mayes told me. "The upper body of the figure was visible, but more in silhouette. I do remember it being very thick and wide-bodied."

As the two men watched, the figure took a "side step" with its right foot, "then crossed over with its left foot" as it turned back towards the woods. In that brief moment its body was fully facing the vehicle, and an arm was clearly visible. Then with one more step, the biped crossed a ditch and disappeared into the darkness. "The figure moved very naturally and smoothly," Mayes noted.

Fig. 1-9: Edge of the Piney Woods
(photo by Lyle Blackburn)

The two men used a night vision monocular to scan the area, but saw no further signs of the strange figure. After an examination of the ground for footprints – of which none were visible – they drove the service roads until daylight. But this was also without luck. As in so many of these cases, Mayes was only afforded a brief glimpse at what has become one of Texas' most enduring, yet perplexing mysteries.

✳✳✳✳✳✳✳✳✳✳✳✳✳

While the majority of Bigfoot reports in Texas originate from the East, this is not to say that interesting sightings haven't been reported elsewhere. In a state as large as Texas, there are numerous tracts of forestlands, swamps, and rivers where large creatures could potentially flourish - or at least travel - beyond the piney thickets. In fact, the earliest suspected Bigfoot case in Texas comes from Lavaca County located in the Gulf Coast Prairies and Marshes region southeast of the Piney Woods. Known as the "Wild Woman of the Navidad," the details were recorded by author J. Frank Dobie in his book, *Tales of Old-Time Texas*.

As the story goes, settlers living near the banks of the Navidad River southeast of Hallettsville began to notice odd, barefoot tracks around their homesteads in the year 1837. These were usually two sets of human-like footprints with one set being larger than the other, as if to suggest a male and female. As time went on, the larger tracks ceased to appear, leaving only the smaller "Wild Woman" tracks, which increased in frequency. Numerous attempts to capture the Wild Woman failed as "she" was apparently able to move with great stealth through the darkness.

Finally, in 1845, the locals resolved to catch the mysterious prowler once and for all. On a moonlit night several hunters on horseback, along with their hounds, took up watch near an area where recent Wild Woman activity had been found. When one of the hunters heard a rustling in the brush, he looked up to see the "thing." He lurched forward on his horse, but the thing took off running toward a heavily wooded area. When his horse finally caught up, the rider tried to lasso it, but was unsuccessful. Once the thing reached the woods, it disappeared within the trees.

The rider said the entity he pursued had long hair, no clothes, and brown fur that covered its entire body. It was also carrying some sort of object, but had dropped it during the pursuit. The hunters later found a five-foot club in the field but no further sign of the Wild Woman. She had simply vanished into the realms of folklore and Bigfoot history.

In the following years, similar Bigfoot-esque reports were documented by newspapers. In 1875, *The Statesman* out of Austin ran an article about a "Wild Boy" who was caught by men on horseback near San Marcos in southern central Texas. The "strange being," who was described as being fearful and aggressive, apparently had a body "covered with hair about four inches long." While it's more likely this was a feral child – possibly suffering from hypertrichosis[4] - its hairy form does raise an eyebrow.

Nearly a century later, in 1964, several people reported seeing a "large, hulking, hairy creature" near Chambers Creek in Ellis County. The Chambers Creek Monster, as it was called, had been reportedly seen by old-timers in the area since at least the 1930s.

In 1963, the *Denton Record-Chronicle* reported that someone near

---

4   Hypertrichosis is a disorder that causes excessive hair growth on the human body.

the town of Denton claimed to have seen a "hairy, eight-foot thing" which the locals referred to as a "monster." The details are sketchy, but curiously, Denton is very close to another area where people would report a Bigfoot-like creature a few years later.

In July 1969, just 40 miles south of Denton, a rash of bizarre sightings grabbed headlines when numerous people claimed encounters with an aggressive and hairy bipedal creature. Dubbed the "Lake Worth Monster," the creature is perhaps the best known in all of Texas Bigfoot lore due to the newspaper coverage and a book of the same name by local author, Sallie Ann Clarke.

The incidents first made the news on July 10, when the *Fort Worth Star Telegram* reported: "Six terrified residents told police… they were attacked by a thing they described as being half-man, half-goat and covered with fur and scales." Although the creature was often described in terms of a "goatman" or even a "scaly goatman," most eyewitness accounts agreed it was large, bipedal and covered in white hair, placing it into the domain of Bigfoot. (Descriptions of white hair are rare among Bigfoot reports, but do occur.)

The following day, on July 11, Jim Marrs of the *Fort Worth Star Telegram* reported that upwards of 30 residents witnessed the creature running along a ridge near Greer Island when it "threw an automobile tire and wheel 500 feet (fig 1-10)."

Several other encounters were reported, some of them violent, along with footprint finds and strange cries coming from the surrounding woods. Given the location was a known lover's lane hangout, the case teeters on urban legend, but regardless the locals insisted the thing was more "monster" than "man." During my research I've interviewed several people involved, including Bill Morris, who was present when the first eyewitnesses called police from a café payphone to report they had been attacked by an unknown creature. He assured me that their fear was real.

Ironically, Lake Worth is located quite close to my childhood home on the outskirts of Fort Worth. This would have surely been my first introduction to possible Bigfoot-like creatures roaming the woods of North Texas if it had not occurred when I was a baby. By the time I saw *The Legend of Boggy Creek* in the mid-1970s, the Lake Worth Monster flap had long since faded from the news, leaving the Fouke

Monster to be the catalyst for my early local interest.

FIG. 1-10: *The ridge near Greer Island*
where the Lake Worth Monster was seen
(photo by Lyle Blackburn)

Other notable reports outside the East Texas Pine Belt include the Horizon City Monster case of 1975 (in which numerous teens claimed to see a hairy, eight-foot-tall creature near El Paso), the Kelly Bigfoot incidents of 1976 (in which two people saw bipedal "Bigfoot type" creatures near San Antonio's Kelly Air Force Base), the Hawley Him case of 1977 (in which several boys saw a "kind of an ape, but still a man" near the Hawley / Abilene area), and the Vidor Werewolf case of 1978 (in which a six-foot, shaggy creature was seen – and hunted – east of Beaumont).

These type of newspaper reports generally dry up by the 1980s, although sightings in and out of the Piney Woods were still collected by Bigfoot researchers during the time, and even reside in my own personal files after having interviewed witnesses about past experiences. More recently there was a case in El Campo, Texas where a couple of people saw a five foot tall, grayish creature. Police were called to the scene, but could find no visible signs of a creature the locals now refer to as the "El Campo Ape Man."

Recent reports from the San Antonio area also suggest ape-like creatures still roam the woods of South Central Texas, but in general, the majority of cases now come from the Piney Woods, whether coincidental or as a result of shrinking woodlands in the central part of the state. Regardless of the cause, there is no doubt the Piney Woods of East Texas lie at the heart of Texas Bigfoot history and ongoing research.

****

Beyond the anecdotal witness reports there have been numerous - and promising - discoveries of hair and footprints over the years. While it's impossible to cover all aspects of the Texas Bigfoot in one chapter (it would truly encompass a complete book), these bits of evidence, when combined with a history of credible witness reports, help strengthen the theory Bigfoot is indeed residing in the Lone Star State. But what kind of Bigfoot?

As we have seen in these example reports, the creatures are often described in terms of being more "ape-like" than the archetypal "Bigfoot" of the Pacific Northwest. For example, they have been seen running on all fours, using their long arms to propel themselves in a fashion similar to known primates. They've been described as eight foot tall giants, but also as smaller creatures ranging from four to seven feet in height.

The height aspect can logically be explained by age, as any animal must grow to maturity. However, the extreme ape-like descriptions demand more consideration. Are these creatures of the same classification (albeit unknown) as the Sasquatch reported in other parts of the country? Are they something completely different, perhaps more related to the Skunk Ape variety said to inhabit Florida? Or are they a related species that has deviated from their Northwest cousins, having spread out and evolved to accommodate new environments?

While only a physical specimen can truly answer these questions, it's possible creatures here could have adapted to life in the Deep South. A principle known as Bergmann's Rule states that species of a larger size are generally found in colder environments and species of a smaller size are found in warmer regions. While this principle, proposed in 1847, is now contested by some, it could explain variations in description of

Bigfoot-like creatures across the U.S. For example, Washington state is undoubtedly different from Texas in terms of climate, landscape, and food source, therefore it's likely any such North American apes found in these respective regions may have deviated from each other over the years. This could be reflected in hair color, hair length, height, weight, and even the tendency to move on four legs.

These details fall squarely into the realm of scientific study, but a study that currently lacks a definitive sample of the creature it struggles to prove. But this does not deter those who don't mind venturing into the aptly named waters of cryptozoology in an effort to solve a mystery that's been plaguing Bigfoot researchers for more than a half century. The eyewitness reports may be scattered, and the evidence sparse in comparison to other forms of mammalian wildlife, but it's enough to keep the quest alive in hopes Bigfoot can one day be proved.

For the little kid who once gazed into the dense Piney Woods unaware that Bigfoot may dwell in its long shadows, these logical questions have become the crux of my research. But somewhere under the scholarly surface, that wonderment still remains. The excitement that one day it's all going to bust wide open, when one of these mysterious giants makes its indelible mark, not only on the Lone Star State, but on the world at large.

Fig. 2-1: *Author's conception of Bigfoot,* © *Linda S. Godfrey*

Linda S. Godfrey

Kettles, Cows and Sasquatch; Bigfoot in Southern Wisconsin

by Linda S. Godfrey

"The way it moved itself...the agility...it was going somewhere with a purpose!"

Commercial driver Tim A. used those words to describe a figure he witnessed on June 24, 2015, at about 3:20 a.m. in rural Wisconsin. As a trucker with over a million certified commercial miles, he was used to seeing humans and various animals along the road. He knew immediately, however, this was something he'd never before encountered. Tim added he was wide awake that perfectly clear night as he headed east on State Highway 11 nearing Gratiot, about seven miles north of the Illinois border.

He also had a good view of the road via the high beams of his 28,000 lb., single axle truck, as he cruised at about forty miles per hour. Suddenly not forty feet ahead of him, a huge, brown-furred creature dashed across the road— in only two bounds —before hurtling out of sight again by leaping into a ditch.

"This thing *dove*," he said in a later phone interview. "A normal person wouldn't dive onto the ground like this unless they were an acrobat." I talked to him just two weeks after the incident, the sight still very fresh in his mind. He described it as having very long arms and legs, with an estimated weight of 400-500 pounds, and no tail. It kept its head down so he couldn't see its face. But he did get a good look at its hands as it emerged upward from a steep slope on the road's right shoulder. "It was crawling up onto the road through the grass," he said. "I saw the hands and they were huge. The feet had fur but it ran flat-footed like a human. The legs on that thing were...wow!"

Tim added that as the creature launched itself up onto the road, the feet came forward and then it took two huge steps. He stated "At the final step, it took a dive down into a steep grade with tall grass leading up to a dairy farm. He dove headfirst with both arms outstretched.

I never saw his face but being that I was only about forty feet from the creature running across the road, my headlights showed full illumination of the body (fig. 2-2)."

Tim did not stop to examine it further. "I didn't want to meet up with it on other terms or have it chase my truck," he told me. "I have seen everything on the side of the road at night, in fifty states and Canada. Caribou, baby elk…and I haven't seen anything like this."

Another trucker working for the same company as a trainee also saw it a little farther down the same road, just a week later. Tim told a supervisor about the sightings, and was surprised at the man's reply. "He said, 'Oh, Bigfoot. They're everywhere,'" said Tim. "For him to say that, there's something going on."

Fig. 2-2: Many witnesses observe Bigfoot running across the road in front of the car.
Original drawing by Linda S. Godfrey for American Monsters; a History of Monster Lore, Legends and Sightings in America, Tarcher/Penguin/Random House, 2014, all rights reserved.

There is something going on, indeed, in Southern Wisconsin, a location probably not high on anyone's list of likely Bigfoot habitats. And that "something" has been happening since at least the mid-1950s, according to my own documentation, which has been ongoing for twenty-four years.

Even though I'm best known for my investigations of sightings of unknown, wolf-like canines described in my 1992 newspaper article titled *The Beast of Bray Road*, I've also documented many reports of encounters with Bigfoot. And although four of my sixteen published books focus on wolf-like creatures, they also include accounts of growing numbers of Sasquatch sightings. Reports from sober, credible people like the one above (for which I owe thanks to author and former Sci-Fi Café owner Mary Sutherland) still regularly find their way to my desk.

Not that it wasn't a surprise when the Bigfoot reports started coming. I was just as astonished as anyone else that these huge, hairy primates appeared to inhabit my home state--not just in the northern woods and wildlife areas, like the enormous, million-and-one-half acre Chequamegon Nicolet National Forest, but in the generally tamer, southern half of the state as well. I'm sure most people wouldn't believe it's possible for a population of giant, human-like primates to subsist in such a well-populated area as southern Wisconsin. But most people don't have an accurate notion of the varied landscape of the southern part of the Dairy State. There are cow pastures, yes, but also many acres of forest, miles of weird and ancient quartz ridges, wide-ranging networks of freshwater lakes and active river systems, not to mention Great Lakes shorelines, and a multi-level topography still in place, courtesy of the last Ice Age glacier. Among the geological formations it left behind are the vast tracts of deep, kettle-shaped depressions and ridges stretching from Walworth County to Sheboygan County. These 56,000 acres are known as various units of the Kettle Moraine State Forest, and they serve as a frequent locale for close brushes with both Bigfoot and dogmen. One elder and anthropologist of the state's Ho-Chunk tribe told me both these creatures lived here long before even the native people arrived.

While I'm not sure exactly how long Sasquatch have been seen in these parts in modern times, tales of sightings of a Bigfoot-like creature known locally as "The Bluff Monster" have circulated around the southern Kettle Moraine since the 1960s (fig. 2-3). Two women who attended Palmyra/Eagle High School in the 1960s told me they and at least a dozen of their classmates saw it on numerous occasions as it ran around the top of a lighted hill near her parent's farm, as if hunting, and that watching it was a regular pastime for her and her friends. She drew a sketch of the creature as she remembered it, and anyone today would recognize her drawing as a Bigfoot. Although those witnesses didn't know it at the time, a similar legend arose in those same years, just 10-15 miles to the southeast of Bluff Road around East Troy, where another woman told me she and her friends called it the "Yeti" or the "Eddy."

Fig. 2-3: Witness sketch of "Bluff Monster" seen by several Palmyra area high school students on various occasions.

Drawing by witness

In July, 1964, a sighting of a Bigfoot by rural Walworth County resident Dennis Fewless made news reports statewide. As detailed by Madison reporter Jay Rath in *The Capital Times* and later, my *The Beast of Bray Road*, Fewless was driving home from a late shift at the Admiral Corporation in Harvard, Illinois between midnight and 1 a.m. and headed north. He had just turned off State Hwy. 89 onto Richmond Township Road west of Delavan when he noticed something very tall and hairy, covered in dark fur, moving in a cornfield on the north side of the road. He told me in an interview I videotaped in 1993, "He jumped a four-and-a-half foot fence, ran across the road and jumped the fence on the other side. Estimated height, seven to eight feet. Estimated weight, 400-700 pounds."

The creature ran on two legs, swinging its arms, said Fewless. "The closest thing it looked like was a large human being. Scared the devil right out of me. It showed no fear, didn't stop, didn't waver. I think it had to be intelligent because it was running 75-100 yards off the main highway, parallel with the highway."

Fewless didn't think it was a hoax. He reasoned it would have made little sense for a human to be running in a cornfield at that time of night with little chance of being seen by anyone, and added he didn't believe a human could have sailed over the fences the way this creature did. He also told me the creature leaned forward as it ran, and he didn't see a tail, snout or ears. The head was rounded and the arms were longer than a human's. "And no, I was not drinking," he said. "I know what I saw."

The Horse Slasher

A few years later, in 1972, another encounter of the Bigfoot kind occurred on a farm about 15-20 miles north of Delavan. This incident was unusual—beyond the fact a person was claiming to have seen a Bigfoot—in that a DNR (Department of Natural Resources) warden actually admitted to me in a phone interview that he believed the witness.

Agent David Gjetson said he had responded to a call from a woman who first reported a tall, hairy, upright, apelike creature was walking around in her farm yard. The creature left quietly, but came back two weeks later. This time it walked up to the front porch of the farmhouse and rattled the doorknob, before scraping its nails across the siding hard enough to leave scratch marks seven feet off the ground. It then headed for her horse barn, entered it and slashed her horse's neck, leaving a 30- inch, non-fatal gash. The woman, terrified and helpless inside her house, heard the horse whinnying in fear. The Bigfoot then left again by way of her garden where it left foot-long tracks. Gjetson said that although he wouldn't reveal the woman's name, he did investigate her property, attested to the horse's injury and scratches on the house siding, and said he thought she was truthful. I've since had numerous other sightings reported in the near vicinity of that farm.

One of those Jefferson area sightings occurred in summer, 1993, when a young man named Andy Hurd saw a Bigfoot lurking in the barn of his family farm on Fromader Road, near Hebron in Jefferson County. He surprised the creature after he ran into the barn as part of a game he was playing with a friend. "It was tall, bigger than any man," he said. "It had a really hairy face and head, and the hair on the neck was thicker. His nose was more like an ape's than a snout. Luckily for Hurd, the beast didn't seem eager for a closer look at him, either. "It ran east through the barn and out…on two feet. It ran crouched over and really fast for being crouched. It was just huge."

Hurd told his parents, who called the sheriff's department. A deputy came to investigate and found items strewn around inside the building, and a large, nest-like circular area tramped down in the grass outside the barn. The deputy told them they had received other reports of a similar creature around Sullivan, a small town about eight miles northeast of Hebron. A body of water known as Rome Pond lies between them, surrounded by marshes, and Fromader Road runs directly into 1500 acres of open marsh and woods, called Princess Point Wildlife Area. I've read various accounts of Bigfoots having been observed digging in marshes elsewhere for cattail roots, which would also serve as an excellent and abundant food source in this area.

More Ditchings

A more recent Jefferson County report occurred in early 2012, when an elderly Rock County couple pulled up to a stop sign at the intersection of Star School Road and State Hwy. 12, just south of Fort Atkinson. The wife riding in the passenger seat happened to look down into the ditch to her right, and to her great surprise saw what she described to me as a reddish-furred Bigfoot lying in the ditch perfectly still and probably hoping no one would notice. She didn't say a word to her husband—she told me he is not a fan of the topic of unknown creatures—but she allowed me to interview her by phone, and said she was quite sure of what she had seen.

Incidentally, in that same year a completely unrelated older woman was driving on a rural road in eastern Walworth County when she noticed a rusty-colored, large, furry being lying just off the road amid some landscaping debris. It was curled almost into a fetal position and was bigger than a human, she said. It also lay stock still as the woman's car passed. She was going slowly enough to get a good look at it, but did not even think about going back for a second peek, she told me.

Hiding in Plain Sight

As long as we're discussing ditch-diving and the "frozen Bigfoot" phenomenon, two simple camouflage methods that will sound familiar to anyone who studies reports of Sasquatch behavior, I have yet a third example of Bigfoot playing possum in southern Wisconsin. This incident occurred in the area of Spring Green, about thirty miles west of Madison, in Sauk County. A woman who asked me to refer to her as L.N. said in the early 2000s, she and her husband were renting a farmhouse situated in a valley between the little towns of Plain and Bear Valley. This part of the state is hilly, bluff country and very close to the Wisconsin River.

She wrote, ominously, "We kept seeing little bits of deer fur on our patio." This unsettling scenario began to progress; first to the couple finding a pile of five or more deer carcasses on a sandstone hill behind the house, and finally to her husband and daughter sighting a large, upright, dark-red-furred creature running through the woods on the property. It gave them a deep, "blood-curdling" growl as it passed near them on their quickly curtailed hike.

The next summer, L.N. was outdoors weeding her garden near a metal-roofed springhouse when she unaccountably heard a voice in her head telling her to go into the house. This was not a normal sort of occurrence for her. She shook it off as her imagination and kept weeding. The next thing she knew, small rocks began to pelt the shed roof from the direction of the woods, and the voice repeated its message more insistently. This time, she ran in the house and locked the door. She told me she didn't know at that time that Bigfoots are famous for throwing rocks.

L.N. said they generally kept these experiences to themselves, especially when talking to friends from Chicago who often came to visit. But later that summer, their Chicago friends arrived one day asking if she and her husband had seen the very tall, hairy statue of some creature L.N.'s neighbors had put in their yard. Neither L.N. nor her husband recalled such a thing, so they all jumped in a car and drove to see. There was no trace of anything remotely resembling a statue.

A Real Stumper

It's interesting that in all three of these examples, the "frozen" creature was described as having dark red, or what I like to call cinnamon-colored hair or fur. It may just be this is a predominant color for Bigfoots in this area, although I've also received many reports of very dark-furred Bigfoots, and several beige-gray or "blond" creatures. I actually believe I've personally seen an individual with smoky black fur playing possum. Let me set a brief bit of background first:

Readers of my blog at *lindagodfrey.com* and my book, *Real Wolfmen*, may recall accounts of my encounter in July, 2012 in a privately owned area of kettle terrain, where it's been my habit to walk for many years. For those unfamiliar with the southern Wisconsin landscape, kettles are the divots and depressions left by the outwash of retreating glaciers. It's hilly, woodsy, and lush. That warm and completely still summer evening at about 7 p.m., while there was still good daylight, I witnessed "something" that was perched about 40 feet up a big, living oak tree growing from near the bottom of a kettle. The creature twisted and snapped an 8-inch diameter, 35-foot long limb from the tree and dropped it to the ground. There was no wind, and no sign of any other humans. I couldn't see the creature because of the foliage on the tree, but I went back half an hour later with my friend Sandra Schwab, and her daughter Natalie. Just as we were preparing to leave, Natalie saw it "striding" behind a bank of greenery in an adjoining kettle. She described it as upright, larger than a human, and covered with beige-gray or blond fur. We also smelled it, found hand-rub marks on the limb, and heard the same type of low, threatening growl described by L.N. before we high-tailed it out of there, still gagging a little on the skunkish, moldy, grass-like odor we could only presume had been emitted by the creature.

Ever since then, I've had various weird experiences anywhere near that area. It almost seems as if local Bigfoots remember me from that incident, and are now aware I'm aware of them. I know some researchers believe the Bigfoot somehow "tag" those who have seen them. I wouldn't go that far—I believe they can simply recognize individual humans—but sometimes I wonder if that first one followed me home. My office windows are often pelted with sticks and small stones when I'm working late at night, and I've heard large body slams against my house at odd times, usually just after sundown. Although my trail cam never seems to get a shot of the creatures no matter what I leave for bait, I've found very wide 15-inch and 8-inch prints, and have caught other glimpses of animals I can't identify as any known animal in various Kettle Moraine areas. I believe one of those glimpses was a Bigfoot caught self-disguising in a frozen pose that resembled a stump.

Fig. 2-4: A trail in the Kettle Moraine State Forest.
Photo by Linda Godfrey, all rights reserved.

It happened in spring, 2013, as I drove past a corn field still bare from the previous fall's harvest except for a few tattered remnants of stalks. The field lay between two kettle woods on a road about half a mile from my tree encounter. Something turned my attention toward the field, and there I noticed a very large, oddly shaped black tree

45

stump sitting about forty feet from the woods, less than half a football field's distance from me. I was driving very slowly because there's a well-used deer and turkey crossing right at that spot. My husband and I have nicknamed it the "wildlife field."

I remember asking myself as I looked both ways for deer, why a farmer would have left such a big stump right in the middle of that cultivated area. And then it hit me, there should *not have been* a stump there. I drive past that field very frequently, and would surely have noticed such a big, misshapen black stump before that moment. As I realized that fact, my car had rolled on far enough that my view of the stump had just been blocked by small trees. I hit the brakes, threw the car in reverse, and then hit the brakes again. I could only stare at the field in disbelief. In just those few moments, the big stump had completely disappeared. If it had been a known animal, I should have seen it running or flying or crawling away. But there was nothing to be seen.

I racked my brain but couldn't think of any other black-colored animal large enough to be what I saw, and fast enough to zip forty feet back into the kettle woods in about two or three seconds. I've often observed turkeys grazing on bits of last year's corn there, but it would have taken at least five of them mashed together in a frozen and unlikely clump to approximate the correct mass, and I still would have seen their legs. A black bear would be the right color and size, and we do have the very occasional bear passing through the county, but I don't think a bear could have or would have scrunched itself into that pose and held it. I did very recently see a black deer in the area, but I would have recognized a deer in any position. But since I *have* read countless other tales of Bigfoot doing exactly what I've just described, the one possibility I can't dismiss is this was indeed a sighting of a 'Squatch playing freeze-frame.

These examples of certain Bigfoot behaviors may seem a bit of a digression from my main topic of Bigfoot in southern Wisconsin, but I do have a relevant point to make. Whether the "statue pose" ploy and ditch-diving actions are instinctive among Bigfoot, or something they learn from one another as a survival skill, these are useful tricks that help explain how such a large creature can sneak around a well-populated area like southern Wisconsin and remain mostly incognito. These tricks seem almost too simple to work, but perhaps the Bigfoots know us more adroitly than we know ourselves.

I have a feeling a huge percentage of passersby on any given road do not scrutinize the scenery as they go, nor would most people think twice about passing an odd stump or any other stationary feature of the landscape. And how many people notice what's in ditches? I must point out the creature witnessed by Tim A. saw also dove headfirst into the ditch. This action is very commonly reported not only in Wisconsin but everywhere Sasquatch is observed. I believe these behaviors are key to the creature's ability to survive wherever there are woods, hills, water and great food, as well as a fair number of annoying humans to avoid at all costs. I also think these basic maneuvers are probably part of a much more complex strategy that is not only effective in keeping their presence secret, but also indicative of high intelligence and the ability to adapt to changing habitats.

Counting Sasquatch

These observations beg the question of how many Bigfoots there might actually be in southern Wisconsin. To my knowledge, no one has yet perfected a foolproof Bigfoot Census. My own sense is that, given my sightings data and the presumption there must be more than I'm personally aware of, it's likely there are several very small family groups operating around Walworth County and the adjoining parts of Rock and Jefferson Counties alone. I have received at least one report--from a very credible source--of a couple of adult Bigfoots seen snatching food from a garbage pile in northern Walworth County as one of them held an infant Bigfoot, and I've also found two prints in different areas that appear to be the size of a juvenile.

The fact there are three different fur colors seen and reported in southern Wisconsin is another indication of variety in the (presumed) local breeding pool. This indicates either a fair-sized Bigfoot population lives here, or there are traveling, single creatures that pass through, but stay long enough to leave some of their genetic material. Alternatively, perhaps there are different family bands that all migrate continuously through the area and none that are permanent.

Our lack of knowledge about them makes it almost impossible, in my view, to say with any degree of certainty how many individuals may be around an area at any time. But we can look at the wide-ranging scope of reports from the Dairy State's southernmost third, and speculate there are probably more than we think there are. As a start, here's a short list of some other incidents besides those already discussed. I'll include only those I've personally investigated. (Some are also recounted in full in my various books.)

- Fall, 1980, Ronald Nixon observed a bipedal, hairy hominid watching him from the shore of the Bark River north of Whitewater, Wisconsin, as he fished from a boat not far from Hebron. Nixon later passed away without telling his encounter to anyone except one relative, who passed it on to me. The relative said he was sitting alone in a shallow area of the river and using a "stinky cheese" bait—which in retrospect may have attracted more than just catfish. He suddenly caught a movement on the nearby shore and saw a huge, dark-colored, hairy creature "hunched over and hulking by the weeds." The figure quickly receded into the shadows, and Nixon left, too. The relative said Nixon entirely gave up his beloved pastime of fishing from that point on.

- Early spring, 1994, David and Mary Pagliaroni, a married couple in their forties, saw a Bigfoot stop only ten feet in front of their car on Honey Lake Bridge. They watched as it made eye contact with them and then placed one hand on the railing and jumped to a creek bed 15 feet below. They agreed its hair was "reddish-brown" and "longish." David said, "The hair came down off the head and formed almost a little mini-cape, you could see where the hair all ended." David also had a very good look at the hand, and noted he was deliberately calling it a hand rather than a paw. "There were fingers and a thumb, it looked like a hand, it wasn't a paw or claw or anything," he said. He added the creature didn't seem to be in a hurry when it did take off. David's testimony was included in the first season episode of the History Channel series *Monsterquest*, titled "American Werewolf" after my book, *Hunting the American Werewolf*, and he passed a polygraph test as part of the show. (The episode did not make it clear that the Pagliaroni's saw a Bigfoot rather than a dogman.)

***Fig. 2-5: Sketch by Honey Lake Bridge Jumper
eyewitness David Pagliaroni.***

- Summer, 1999, a Chicago computer salesman named Joe was driving to North Lake one mile north of Millard, on County Road O, to fish at dawn when he noticed movement through the passenger side window. He saw a 7-foot, 400-pound creature swinging its long arms as it walked along the ditch, pitched slightly forward. It was covered in unkempt, cinnamon-colored fur, which also obscured the entire face.

There were no ears or muzzle he could see. Joe told me his first thought was, "Whoa, that's not a person," and his second was, "Don't stop the car." He kept the sighting to himself for years until he accidentally found me online. I think it's interesting that in this case, the Bigfoot did not seem to feel the need to flatten itself in the ditch and just kept striding along.

- March, 2005, a University of Wisconsin-Whitewater student saw a Bigfoot cross Highway 59 near Lima Marsh in Rock County as she drove home from her job at a movie theater late at night. She said she had a good enough look at it in her headlights to be sure of what she saw.

- April, 2005, restaurant owners Lenny and Stacie Faytus saw a seven-foot tall, 350-pound Bigfoot cross McCord Road in Rock County and dive into a ditch. The creature was covered in brown fur, they said, and needed only two long strides to cross the 20-foot wide road. They said it had a "humanoid" face, no muzzle, and was so hairy they couldn't see any ears or neck. They kept driving and when they reached the spot where the creature should have been, realized it had gone into the deep roadside ditch and probably was lying there prostrate. They never reported it to the authorities.

- Sept., 2005, twenty-two year old Matt Wakely saw a Bigfoot-like creature watching him drive by while it stood just inside a pioneer cemetery at the intersection of White Pigeon Road and Cty. Hwy. B near Pell Lake. It stood with one large foot casually propped atop an old headstone, said Wakely, who added that although it was tall and shaped like a human, its body was covered with brown, shaggy hair. Its head sported an especially wild shock of hair that stood away from its scalp, and it had a round face with a flat, wide nose. Wakely called his mother and said he'd just seen a cave man. Wakely was one of the group of witnesses (along with David Pagliaroni) featured on *Monsterquest* who successfully passed professionally administered polygraph tests.

Fig. 2-6: Original witness Sketch of creature Matt Wakely described as "like a caveman" after it watched him drive past a cemetery near the Wisconsin/Illinois state line in SE Walworth County.

Sketch by Matt Wakely.

*Fig. 2-7: Artist conception of creature Matt Wakely described
as "like a caveman" after it watched him drive past a cemetery near
the Wisconsin/Illinois state line in SE Walworth County.*
Author sketch by witness direction

- April, 2008, a self-described hunter, scientist and outdoorswoman watched as a huge, dark-furred, tailless creature pulled itself up a steep bank off Antique Road in Eagle, Waukesha County, using mainly its long forelimbs. She noted it seemed "confident" and moved easily.

- July 15, 2010, a 51-year old Jefferson County woman saw a 6-7 foot, 250-pound Bigfoot run up a slope and into some trees in daylight on State Hwy. 106 east of Fort Atkinson at Jaeckel Road. It was covered in black fur, she told me, except for a grayish area around its stomach. It had long arms hanging down by its sides, legs like those of a gorilla, and a head it kept bowed as it hunched forward while running. The head seemed too small for its body, she added. There was no tail. She pulled over hoping for a closer look, and added she would have followed it except she had a young child in the back seat.

- September, 2011, a northeastern Rock County woman saw a Bigfoot in a field adjacent to her home at about 10 pm, illuminated clearly by a yard light. She was outdoors at the time and only about 30 feet away, so she heard it clearly as it growled and showed its large but human-like teeth. She scrambled up a rocky embankment to get to the nearest door on her house.

- Summer, 2015, three women driving on a rural road in eastern Walworth County saw a dark-furred, huge, human-like figure rise up out of a field as they passed. They turned around and drove past it again and saw it a second time, but this time the driver also looked in her rear view mirror and witnessed a second, similar creature dashing across the road behind them.

Where Do They Go From Here?

Again, this list is far from exhaustive, but I hope it will serve to give at least a hint of the continued presence of Bigfoot as consistently seen by a very diverse group of witnesses for over five decades in southern Wisconsin. I'm convinced there are far more incidents waiting to be confessed or uncovered, and many more will occur, since it seems to me these enigmatic creatures show every indication they're here to stay.

They are not mere phantoms. No matter what theory of Bigfoot origin a person believes—relict but unknown natural primate, nature spirit or something from another dimension—most witnesses agree they possess solid and impressive physical bodies at least part of the time. The tree limb I saw ripped from that oak in the kettle, for instance, required enormous strength to twist it, snap it, and then toss it down as if it were a twig.

It goes without saying such powerful physical bodies require food and suitable habitat. No problem there, either. All of southern Wisconsin (and northern Illinois) offers a fabulous array of plant and animal life for a Bigfoot's dining pleasure, with the added attraction of cornfields, plentiful water and farms that offer feed mash, warm barns, and even fresh milk. Most of my own sightings and experiences in the southern Kettle Moraine area have occurred around the time black raspberries and mulberries ripen. It's an omnivore's paradise. Why couldn't at least a few Sasquatch live here just as easily as they are said to do in, say, the Pacific Northwest?

That question is probably moot, however, until someone can answer the bigger bone of contention as to whether these creatures exist—not just in Wisconsin but around the world—and can include them as a part of what most people would agree upon as reality. There is no doubt in my mind that they do. Between my own experiences and those of the great number of eyewitnesses I've come to know personally, I don't see how it could be otherwise. My conclusion is Bigfoot's existence in southern Wisconsin is real but as yet imperfectly understood, and bitter-sweet in its implications. Although every Bigfoot researcher dreams of the day Bigfoot may finally be publicly acknowledged, I'm not sure such an announcement would be in the best interest of the creatures. Humanity does not have a great record of playing well with others.

No matter what part of the country, the unknown numbers of Bigfoot may be presently and expertly colonizing. That is only my gut, intuitive feeling as to what they're doing. Bigfoots simply might be better off sticking to those ditches, hiding out in their branch assembly huts, and freezing in place every time a carload of nosy people comes along. I think they know their strange lives likely depend upon it.

Fig. 3-1: Author & Researcher David Weatherly
Credit: David Weatherly

Big Man on the Reservation

by David Weatherly

The man described the creature as being at least eight feet tall with long, dark brown hair all over its body. According to the witness, the shaggy creature's arms swung when it walked and it loped almost like a gorilla. The face was framed in fur, but the features, nose, eyes and mouth, could all be seen clearly. The facial skin was dark and almost leathery. In an easy step, the hairy man stepped over the corral fence and made its way into the underbrush at the edge of the property. Quickly slipping into a grove of trees, the creature escaped from the site in a few easy strides. When first spotted, it had been raiding a plastic bin filled with feed for livestock, and the witness had been alerted by the noise from his nearby horses.

"They were whinnying loud like they do when something has them upset, I came out of the house and there was this big, hairy man dipping in the feed bin."

The report could easily be one of the numerous accounts that come out of Bigfoot hotspots such as Washington, Oregon or Northern California.

This particular report however, comes to us from the heart of the American southwest, deep in the territory of a tribal people who have long known of the existence of these giant ape-like men.

The Navajo Landscape

In the heart of the southwest of the United States lies the largest American Indian reservation in the country. The Navajo Nation covers 27,425 square miles, with portions of the reservation in northeastern Arizona, northwestern New Mexico and southeastern Utah. As is the case with all Native reservations, the land is managed via agreements with the US Congress and treated as a sovereign, semi-autonomous Indian nation.

Tribal numbers in 2011 showed a population of 300,048 people.

The Navajo Nation has one of the largest tribal governments of North American Indian tribes and includes a large law enforcement division.

The terrain is rugged yet beautiful, fitting the common idea of the Wild West with sweeping vistas, towering rocks and earthy colors. But there's more, much more. There are lakes and rivers providing fresh water. Steep mountains are covered with trees, and in the winter, snow. There are ancient ruins, some unseen by humans for years and deep cave systems, potential shelter for all manner of creatures.

Some areas are so remote they're only accessible by four or even six-wheel drive vehicles in difficult weather.

For an area so large (bigger than ten of the US states) few people are very familiar with it. Travelers often pass through, stopping to take a photo of the majestic "Ship Rock," but otherwise paying little attention to what appears to be a stark landscape.

By all appearances, the Navajos mostly keep to themselves. Their culture is complex and ancient, with great importance placed on clan membership and family.

Traditionally, members of the tribe aren't open about supernatural topics and many aspects of their culture, the discussion of witchcraft and skinwalkers is taboo. Times are changing though, and many Navajos are finally starting to open up a bit. In recent years, some tribal members have taken the radical step of becoming investigators themselves, openly talking about topics like Bigfoot, skinwalkers and pursuing cases in order to find the truth behind old legends.

In the midst of all of this, the big hairy man has gotten a lot of attention.

To tribal members, he is "Ye'e'iitsoh," a Navajo word that loosely translates to "huge monster." But there are other terms, too. "Yei Tso" meaning "great giant" and "Yei Men." These days more often than not natives simply use the term Bigfoot like much of the rest of the country does.

In general Bigfoot sightings on the Navajo reservation seem to come in waves. 1973 saw a number of reports as did 1989. In recent years the clusters have been even closer together. From 2011 on, reports have been fairly steady with a few dips in numbers here and there.

Fig. 3-2: The Navajo Nation, Four Corners Region

Some of the increase in reports is likely due to the new attitude of openness developing among the Navajo themselves. It's likely the numbers will continue to grow since there are now numerous groups on reservation land actively investigating sightings.

Historical Encounters

Despite the usual, traditional reluctance of the Navajo to report such matters, over the years there have been some interesting accounts of Bigfoot on the reservation. Just going back to the 1960s, we find a few of note that give a clear sense that some kind of bipedal creature has been wandering around the desolate grounds of the Navajo nation for a long time, and the locals were well aware of its presence.

Sasquatch researcher John Green had a contact in the region and included some interesting reports in his books. From "The Sasquatch File" we get an encounter from the late 1960s. The sighting is reported to have taken place in the Chuska Mountains of New Mexico: *"Mrs. Chessman wrote that two Navajo sheepherders shot at a "bear" almost eight feet tall that ran on its hind legs. Wounded, it ran with great leaps on its hind legs into a deep canyon where two others came out of the brush to help it."*

Another report from Green's contact, Mrs. Chessman, reported on a direct sighting by a Navajo family who encountered what they described as a "gorilla standing upright."

Chuska Mountains, Arizona, about 1967: *"Mrs. C.A. Chessman, Farmington, New Mexico, wrote me that a Navajo family having a picnic saw an animal looking like a gorilla standing about 200 feet away watching them. It was on its hind legs and parted the underbrush with its hands. When they noticed it, it turned and walked off."*

In the same book Green lists other encounters the Navajo were having in the Chuska mountain region. Apparently, at least through the 1970's, there were reports of these Bigfoot-like creatures stealing livestock from tribal members.

Chuska Mountains, New Mexico, 1971: *"Mrs. Chessman wrote to me that a friend told her that upright "bears" were taking sheep out of corrals in the mountains by reaching over the fence. The friend had seen one walking with sticks on its arm."*

"A trader at Cortez, Colorado told me that he had been told by a trader at Sheep Springs that the Navajo were having trouble with "bears" that walk on their hind legs" stealing sheep out of corrals."

Continuing with some older sightings, we have one from *The Arizona Republic* on February 11, 1979, where a Mr. Outah told the newspaper about a sighting of a Bigfoot near a local church: *"The thing disrupted church services by causing every dog in the village to begin barking simultaneously. Police were called and found smears of fresh blood on a church bus and large human-like footprints which led through a wash and....disappeared where First Mesa's sheer cliff walls make their precipitous rise. Another man said he heard strange noises at night similar to a woman's screams. When he went to investigate, he saw a "very large and hairy living thing standing near a tree. Another witness said the creature had a head as large as a pumpkin."*

It seems that 1979 was an active year for the hairy creatures. The BFRO's (Bigfoot Field Researchers Organization) online database contains an account from the same year posted by a man who lived near Fort Defiance. The man had an experience in his youth when he was eleven, and an identical incident three years later just before his fourteenth birthday.

While playing outside with friends he stated he heard "a terrible scream that lasted for about fifteen minutes on and off." He states in his report: *"Now at the time I remember there being reports of giant Yei Men taking sheep from corals, but I didn't believe until that night. The time must have been about 12 PM. What is ironic about this incident is that it did not only happen once but twice, three years later in the same conditions. And there were low-key rumors at the time. Now this hasn't bothered me but I sure would like to know how it ever wandered into our region, for a fact."*

The witness has a bit more to say about the "Yei Men," stating his grandmother told him about a "big man" taking one of her sheep out of her corral by simply stepping over the fence one night. He also mentions the tribe's oral history of the creatures: *"In our oral history our elders spoke of Yei Men of whom will come and take you away if you're bad. I mean just put two and two together. Now this had to be a Bigfoot, because on several recordings the sounds are identical to what we heard that night!"*

The witness states that in total about six people were with him and heard the sounds that night.

Author Philip L. Rife ran across an account from 1980 and reported it in his book, "Bigfoot Across America." The account comes from New Mexico and involves a Navajo family living near the town of Toadlena in San Juan County. Here they experienced a series of strange incidents around their property. One family member reported: *"The dogs would bark at something unseen to us, and the sheep would run away from something hidden in the forest. We would feel like something was watching us from the shadows."*

The incidents became more frightening once family members began to catch glimpses of the "something" that was watching them. At supper time one evening a member of the family burst into the home in a panic. According to the report, the man: *"...came running in crying and white as a sheet. He was always the macho type that showed no emotion, so to see him this frightened alarmed (us) to hurry out the door.*

I saw something down at the well. I first thought it was a black bear. Then I noticed it was a grayish-brown color and kneeling. I never heard of a bear that could kneel like a man. It looked as if it was washing something off or taking a drink. I had no problem with it until it looked over its shoulder at us, and I could see its features, man-like."

These reports represent but a small sampling of accounts from the past fifty years or so, but common themes emerge. The propensity of the creatures to raid corrals and the theft of livestock. The large size of the beings and the fearful reactions of those who encounter them, and the frequent implication they are not alone.

More contemporary reports give us further details, especially in recent years, since more people are interested in trying to glean every bit of information possible from the accounts. In fact in modern times law enforcement officers are often involved which leads to a whole new level of data collection, observation and credibility.

Enter the Rangers

Modern interest in Bigfoot has led to the formation of a lot of research groups around the country, and the Navajo Nation has not been left out. The number of natives willing to discuss their encounters has continued to grow, and some have become quite active in the pursuit of the creature. But a unique group has taken over some of the field work in the reservation. The Navajo Rangers.

According to a CBS news report from 2012, it all started around 2002 when officials on the Navajo Reservation decided to stop the snickering and to treat witnesses to strange events with respect and dignity. Instead of ignoring the reports, thorough investigations would be carried out. And when the call was put out to law enforcement, one agency stepped up to take the challenge, the Navajo Nation Rangers.

The Navajo Rangers are a federal law enforcement resource. They manage national parks, archaeological sites, fish and wildlife services and more. According to retired Lieutenant John Dover, the Rangers deal with a lot of Bigfoot related reports. Dover cites one case in particular that had thirty witnesses who saw a creature they described as a Bigfoot. At eight feet in height it easily stepped over a barbed wire fence and escaped the scene. Dover was later on the scene and reports: *"We came out with physical evidence. Hair samples, footprints, stride distances, logs that had been pulled out of the bog area and removed— normal people wouldn't have been able to do that."*

Dover now speaks publicly about some of the strange cases he investigated over the years as part of the Rangers. Sergeant Stanley Milford, Jr. usually accompanies him as co-lecturer and the pair easily hold audience's attention with their accounts of hauntings, UFOs and Bigfoot on the reservation.

In terms of the hairy cryptid, Milford emphasizes the isolated lives of some of the people who call the Rangers to report incidents, and how much the encounters affect them: *"Imagine an elderly person, living in a remote area encountering one of these things. It can be a frightening, life-changing experience."*

Dover and Milford have been on countless locations investigating sightings of the creatures, and they've heard a wide range of complaints from livestock theft to "window peeking."

One case they cite yielded a long trackway of large prints: *"The stride was five feet —five feet between the prints— that's a long stride, and it went up the side of a hill that was about a forty-five degree angle. This thing had no difficulty climbing that steep hill."*

There are supernatural elements to many of these tales. Some Navajo say they have seen the hairy man show up at ceremonial gatherings, lurking around the edges of the sacred space, yet vanishing into thin air when people try to look at him too closely.

Ranchers in the Fluted Rock area of Arizona say they know about the creature, and they blame him for the sheep kills they find, since the animals are often obvious victims of predator attacks, and a lifetime of ranch living has taught them more than anyone the differences in predator kills. These ranchers know when their stock has fallen prey to mountain lions, coyotes or poachers - or something else.

Some natives retell stories passed down by their families, more evidence for the long standing tradition of this creature's existence on the land of the Navajo, but the Rangers put their focus on the physical evidence along with the eyewitness accounts. Their goal is to help the people they serve deal with the situation as best they can.

While the Rangers set the precedent for dealing with cases outside the scope of normal criminal activity, other agencies on the reservation get their share of reports too. One case in particular made waves on television several years ago.

The Crownpoint Howler

Crownpoint is a quiet little reservation town with just under three thousand residents. In recent years it has been plagued by an eerie sound. Most often heard between the hours of midnight and two A.M., the disturbing cry puts locals on edge.

Community members are well familiar with the sounds of known wildlife and they say this noise is unlike anything they've heard before. A long, moaning cry that rouses people from their beds and causes the hair on the back of their necks to stand up.

According to local hunter Bobby Alviso, the sound is not that of animals commonly found in the area such as coyotes, elk and wild dogs. Alviso says when he first heard the sound it was a long, drawn out wail, a single sound. It stopped, and when it started again moments later, it sounded more like a woman crying out, but it wasn't human. Alviso is confident it's some unknown creature but he's not sure what it is. He says he knows many people in the area who have heard the unsettling cry and they all find it disturbing: *"You hear it, sends chills down the spine of a lot of people, and the way I hear it from my neighbors and my wife, they don't want to hear it again."*

Another area woman described the disturbing sound this way: *"It starts out as a very low, raspy growl and ends up like a big man yelling. It sounds like something in pain. There's something human about it, but not quite."*

The unearthly sound was first reported in July of 2011. It continued throughout most of the year, but in recent times reports have become more sporadic. Locals dubbed the unknown creature "The Crownpoint Howler" and the eerie sound it emits was captured on audio by a professional film crew.

In 2011 the NatGeo channel filmed a series titled "Navajo Cops." The reality program followed officers around the reservation while they dealt with a variety of calls in the vein of the successful reality show "Cops."

Law enforcement is quite different on the Navajo reservation though. To begin with the force is small, only a couple of hundred officers for the entire reservation. Civilian support staff helps with operations, but the end result leaves an approximate 1.9% police officers per one thousand people. Even worse, each officer is responsible for patrolling seventy square miles of reservation land and usually does so alone.

There are cultural differences too. Since the Navajo culture contains many supernatural elements, the police department regularly fields calls about witchcraft, skinwalkers, and large hairy men.

The NatGeo show depicted officers dealing with some of these supernatural based reports, including accounts of the Crownpoint howler in an episode appropriately titled "Eyes of the Howler."

The police department's official policy is to investigate supernatural based cases, so after countless calls and texts to the department complaining about the sound, officers decided to look into exactly what was disturbing the residents of Crownpoint.

Reviewing all the complaints, officers searched the Internet for animal sounds to play for witnesses for comparison to what they were hearing. The hope for an easy answer was abandoned when locals said the sound most closely compared with a recording officers played of a purported Bigfoot scream.

Puzzled and intrigued, the department decided to launch a full investigation, setting up a listening post in the area in an attempt to capture the sound themselves and hopefully solve the mystery.

Captain Steve Nelson and a Lieutenant Begay monitored the post but failed to capture anything on their first attempt. Begay also tried playing the recording of the Bigfoot call, but it too failed to generate a response.

Since so many residents continued to report the disturbance, a second investigation was launched six weeks later, this time during daylight hours. A canyon in the Crownpoint area was identified as the spot locals believed the creature lived. The area is rocky and the canyon contains numerous caves, potential hiding spots for all sorts of creatures, perhaps even a Bigfoot.

During further interviews with locals, police officers uncovered reports of dogs in the area being mauled by some unknown attacker. Investigators also discovered strange footprints in the area around the canyon, and the daylight investigation yielded some other surprising results.

Navajo officers along with the NatGeo film crew staked out an area around the horseshoe-shaped canyon and set the cameras rolling. During the course of filming a weird howl was captured on the film's audio. Officers and film crew alike heard, and reacted to, the strange moan. No one present could identify the sound as a known animal.

Further investigation by the officers revealed several odd finds. Bark was torn off of a nearby tree but there were no signs of a bear or other animal that may have stripped the bark. Those present at the location also experienced a foul odor permeating the area. This odor was strongest on the rocks leading to the canyon's cave system. Additionally, the film crew caught eye shine from something, or someone, just inside the entrance to one of the caves. By the time an officer made the climb up the rocky embankment to check the cave, it appeared to be empty. Whatever had been watching the officers and film crew had made its escape, possibly deeper into the cave system.

Further follow up was delayed due to an urgent call that required officers to abandon the search. Currently the identity of the Crownpoint howler remains a mystery, though reports do continue to come in.

Bigfoot on the San Juan

Just as things were starting to quiet down a bit in Crownpoint, strange activity was on the rise well to the north in a New Mexico riverside town.

Upper Fruitland is a small community in the northeast section of the reservation. The town lies in a beautiful area on the high banks of the San Juan River. With a population of only around three thousand, it's considered one of the most desirable places to live on the reservation.

In recent years residents of the town have had more than their fair share of Bigfoot activity. In fact a 2014 report published in *The Navajo Times* highlights just how much people talk about the subject of Bigfoot: *"Since Audie Greybear came to Upper Fruitland as chapter manager in June, he's had a steady procession of locals in and out his door.*

"They want to tell me about the community's history, they want to tell me about problems they're having—and..." he said, "...They want to talk about Bigfoot."

Meet with a couple of Upper Fruitlanders, and within five minutes or so, the conversation turns to Bigfoot. Everybody seems to have had an encounter—either a glimpse out of the corner of their eye, missing crops or animals, or hearing an eerie, unidentifiable howl in the middle of the night."

Area resident John Blueyes, former director of the Navajo Nation's Agriculture Department, is well aware of the presence of Bigfoot in the area. Taking reporters from *The Navajo Times* out on a tour of the community, he reiterates comments from Audie Greybear about the large number of accounts heard from locals: *"On the tour, we encountered a young man casing the riverbank with a BB gun. As an experiment, Blueyes asked him if he had ever seen Bigfoot roaming near the river.*

He hadn't, but he had heard him.

"One night, about 2:30 in the morning, I was parked somewhere near here in my car and I heard this weird howl," the man volunteered. "It sounded human, but really, really loud. You could hear it echo off the banks."

"See?" Blueyes asked as we pulled away. "Everybody here has a Bigfoot story."

Blueyes himself once saw an extremely tall, shadowy figure walking right down a street in his NHA subdivision at dusk as Blueyes was watering his lawn.

"I thought it was a drunk at first," he said. "But it cocked its head in this really weird, not-quite-human way."

Reporting on Bigfoot activity in Upper Fruitland isn't new for *The Navajo Times*. In an article from 2012, the paper ran a piece on sightings focused on Native researcher Brenda Harris. Harris reported on a number of encounters around her home that included finding a pair of 18-inch long footprints in her yard in 2008. She measured and photographed the prints to keep a record of the incident. Not long after the find there was another, more dramatic incident. Times reporters chronicled her account of the strange episode: *About a week went by before the next encounter. Harris's sister came by at about 10:30 p.m.*

"I could hear the dogs going nuts, but not in the usual way when someone comes over," Harris recalled. "You can tell when something is really disturbing your dogs."

Harris and her sister went out to investigate.

"We could hear something...heavy steps coming toward us," Harris said. "I said, 'Let's climb over the fence.'"

They heard the steps again, and then they saw a shape rise out of the gloom.

"Huge," said Harris. "Very, very hairy...long dark hair and no neck. Kind of a pointy head. The chest was really wide, very muscular. It dropped down on all fours and started running that way. It was surprisingly fast."

Worried about the presence of the creature, Harris spoke with neighbors and found that others had seen the hairy figure too, they were just reluctant to talk about it.

Not one to back down, Harris told her story at the next community chapter meeting and announced that anyone who wanted to speak about their own encounters were welcome to contact her. Not expecting much of a response, she was more than surprised at the number of people who approached her in the aftermath of her public statement.

Since then she has continued to gather accounts, and whenever possible, evidence of the area Bigfoot. Harris believes the creatures live in caves and travel between the mountains north of Hogback to the San Juan River, taking corn and melons from fields along the way. She has made a number of strange finds in the region, including a 300 pound ram with its head literally torn from its body and various biological samples.

She has worked with the Farmington, New Mexico based Crypto Four Corners organization, and has also sent samples to labs for analysis. No results have been publicly posted at this point.

Since there was so much interest Harris formed an organization, the "Shadow Seekers," to pursue reports of the big, hairy creatures. Her group's goal she says, is not to prove that the creatures exist, but to ensure that people stay safe in an area so active with encounters: *"You have the "Finding Bigfoot" show, different shows, and you have researchers from all over the world that are doing research on Bigfoot... But what about the safety of the people? Because we don't know enough about what this creature is capable of doing. That's why I'm here. I don't want to hear about anybody getting hurt."*

Harris says most local authorities don't give much credence to many reports, chalking them up to wild dog or bear sightings. She says the San Juan River basin is an area of high Bigfoot activity and her group spends time patrolling it and other "hot zones" where sightings are most common.

Harris says the creatures will raid gardens for watermelons, onions, potatoes and other edibles. She advises people to be careful about items like animal feed and encourages locals to set up lights around their homes and to keep an eye on their animals, stating: *"If your horses start snorting, there's something out there that shouldn't be."*

Over the years Harris has had many encounters and perhaps her most disturbing was her first. It was the mid-1990s and her husband had gone to work on a graveyard shift, leaving her at home with their children. Harris's younger brother was also at the house. She heard noises outside, coming through the open windows, then she saw the front door knob turning back and forth. Harris heard her dogs under the porch whimpering. She reports: *"I got brave enough finally. I could hear it let go of the screen door. I hurried up and swung open the door, and I just saw this tall black figure with hair from head to toe."*

Harris was positive she had encountered a Bigfoot.

"I've always known that it's been out there."

Native Researchers

Harris is an example of the initiative some Navajo have taken in the attempt to gather information on the strange incidents taking place on their land, and she's not alone in her efforts.

In 2013 she teamed up with actor Jesus "Jesus Jr." Payan to host the first Northern New Mexico Bigfoot and Paranormal Conference. Payan, who has appeared in the television series "Breaking Bad" and several movies, has a long standing interest in cryptids and the paranormal. Payan worked with several different groups investigating reports and presented at the conference himself, lecturing on his theory of the origins of Bigfoot.

Around 300 people showed up for the two day conference. A good turnout for a native-based event about Bigfoot in New Mexico. Attendees were able to hear speakers from around the country offer their views. Additionally, it was a great networking opportunity for those who have had experiences themselves.

Fruitland local Deb Yazzie was in attendance and has been tracking reports of howls, footprints and sightings of the creatures since 2008. In that time she's pinpointed 73 different locations for Bigfoot incidents, and that's a drop in the bucket when data other researchers have been collecting is added into the mix.

Many Native research groups are spending their time out in the field, not just following up on sightings, but actually camping and spending time in hot zones in an effort to have more experiences themselves.

Navajo Fred Eaton has been investigating Bigfoot on the reservation for some time. He says his group frequently experiences rock throwing incidents as well as growls from the creatures. This type of behavior is often reported in other areas of the country and is considered by many researchers to be an aggressive display, likely a display of territorial behavior as the creatures feel their space is being intruded on by humans.

Eaton has been interested in Bigfoot since he was a small child and witnessed one of the creatures peering through his window at night in 1973. Although he was only five years old at the time, the experience stuck with him and led him to explore reports and sightings around the reservation as he grew to adulthood. Over the years he's had other experiences, including another "window sighting" in 2005.

On a summer night as he lay in bed, he turned his head to the right and saw a hairy creature, eight to nine feet tall, peering at him through the window. Eaton says the window was close enough for him to reach out and touch it, and due to the bright moonlight he got a good look at the being. He describes it as having large lips and a heavy, Neanderthal-like brow.

Eaton and his associates currently conduct research and expeditions on the Navajo reservation looking for further evidence of Bigfoot. He believes most people on the "rez" know and accept the existence of the creature on their land.

One thing of particular note, Eaton says there are a lot of accounts that mention creatures in the ten to twelve foot range. While this sounds extreme to some researchers, it is a frequent claim from those investigating Bigfoot on Navajo land. Perhaps there's something in the desert air that makes these things grow taller.

Four Corners Cryptozoologists

Perhaps the group that has done the most extensive research in the region is the organization known as Crypto Four Corners (C4C). This group of Cryptozoologists has both native and non-native members alike and years of collective experience between them.

C4C founder JC Johnson states: *"When you think of New Mexico and the Four Corners, most people won't think of Sasquatch, they think all those types of creatures are up in the rainforest of the Pacific Northwest. But we have constant reports here, and this region has a long, long history of sightings. There's plenty of habitat to support these creatures, and if you can get the locals to talk, they'll tell you that the furry ones are here."*

Fig. 3-3: C4C Researcher JC Johnson.
Credit: JC Johnson

One of the key, active members of the Crypto Four Corners organization is native Leonard Dan. He too, points out stories of Bigfoot on the reservation go way back.

"Oh yes, they have been here for a very long time." Dan states. *"…I*

asked some of the elders, what is Bigfoot? They said, 'oh, those things have been around here for centuries here in our area.'"

As an elder Dan has many tales to tell of traditional views of Bigfoot. He also stays physically active, getting out in the field with other members of the team whenever he can. Often there are those golden moments when Dan will relate tribal stories of the creatures. Dan related one particularly fascinating account by the fireside back in 2007. It was the first time he had told the story. The Crypto Four Corners organization finally released the video of the account in 2014. It involves what many believe was an abduction of a child by Bigfoot. In Dan's own words: *"They say one time that, this family, they were starving. This was way back. I guess they had no food and there was hardly no game that year and what happened was, they were gathering nuts, piñon nuts in this area well southeast of here. They call it Sanostee, that's kind of a hot area too.*

This woman left her little baby in a cradle board against a tree and I guess something got that baby and took it and they looked everywhere for it. They even got these trackers to come in here and look for it. What they say was a bear took it with the cradle board and everything. My grandfather told me this story, he said a big being took that baby. What they did was raise this little girl.

One day, this guy was riding his horse in the mountains, looking for his horses I guess and he came across this little girl sitting under a juniper tree. She was all naked and had long hair, stringy hair. She was about ten years old by then. From being an infant all the way to ten years old, that's how long she was missing.

This Navajo guy, he tried to talk to her saying 'Hi how are you? Are you lost? What's your name?' That little girl, she didn't talk Navajo or anything, she just whooped and grunted noises.

He took her and brought her back down, they had a big meeting and they said, okay, whose little girl is this and the mother, she recognized her right away because her little girl had a birthmark on her shoulder. That's how she knew it was her missing baby.

And everybody was happy that she had returned but they couldn't communicate with her."

Dan says despite constant attempts by tribal members to communicate with the girl, the only responses they could elicit from her were a series of whooping sounds and animalistic grunts.

The girl was sent to school in hopes she could be educated and taught to speak the Navajo language. The girl's mother reported the child continued to have a wild nature and would frequently make whooping sounds deep into the night.

Dan himself encountered the girl in her teenage years when he was in high school. He reports there was something unusual about her: *"My friend pointed her out and told me that little girl, she was taken by something, a creature, and those creatures, they raised her and she couldn't talk.*

And I said, Oh really? I looked at her and I was staring at her and she turned around and looked at me and I just kind of smiled.

She was a nice looking young lady by then, she was sort of pretty, but you could tell, there was a wildness about her and that something didn't look right.

My friend said she was abducted by those wild animals and those animals they raised her."

Dan recognized the account from the story his grandfather had told him. It's unknown what ultimately happened to this "wild child." By all accounts she never revealed anything about her experience living in the wild, or what exactly had abducted her and held her for all those years.

Dan has set a great example that puts him at the forefront of the changing attitude among Navajos. The more people are willing to speak out about their experiences, the more data can be collected and progress made.

The Crypto Four Corners organization has generated a lot of attention over the years and the wide range of researchers involved with the group lead to a lot of accounts and information being collected.

George Harvey and Nicholias Begay, research members of Crypto Four Corners, investigated a series of Bigfoot sightings near the San Juan River in 2015. A young boy was outside of his home playing basketball in the backyard when he noticed a dark figure in the rocks nearby. The figure appeared to be watching the young man, so he alerted his father to the presence of the creature. The boy's father snapped some photos with his cell phone, but unfortunately the camera was only a 1.1 mega pixel so there's not a lot of definition to the images.

Harvey and Begay interviewed the witnesses and found them both believable. The investigators then searched the area for any signs of the reported creature. Although the terrain was too rocky for evidence of footprints, the area did yield some interesting finds.

A large ravine behind where the creature was spotted had a lot of trampled brush. The area offers decent cover and amongst the signs they found, the investigators believe some type of animal or creature had been sleeping in the area. There's also a natural spring that runs along the ravine which would provide fresh water, a vital necessity for any animal in the region. Based on many similar reports, Harvey and Begay believe the creatures like to watch human activity, and the bluff and rocky area would be an ideal spot for this as it offers a good vantage point to view both nearby homes and the highway.

As a member of the C4C organization, George Harvey investigates a lot of reports on the reservation, but he doesn't have to go far to collect regular reports. There have been numerous sightings, literally in his own backyard. George himself has seen the creatures on several occasions. At one point he observed what he describes as an adult and two juvenile Bigfoot walking towards the mesa behind his home. The mesa itself is at a steep angle, but the creatures had no difficulty traversing the steep ascent all the way to the top. Harvey believes the creatures were headed for a nearby cornfield and orchard to gather food. He also reports incidents of rocks being thrown down on his home and property, a common report in areas believed to be inhabited by Bigfoot.

Johnson, Harvey and other members of C4C have been busy gathering hair and tissue samples for a DNA study. Previously the group submitted samples to the Ketchum project, but due to the controversial results they decided to conduct their own independent study.

One of the more stunning reports of Bigfoot on the reservation comes from Harvey's sister Alex, who had her own encounter with some of the hairy creatures. A report filed with Lon Strickler's website Phantoms and Monsters, provides details of the sighting: *"George's sister Alex, recalls an encounter she had on January 4, 2015 with a group of 'furry ones'…part of a larger habituation group that migrates throughout the area. Alex was driving a four-wheeler on the homestead, along with her dogs, when she encountered several huge figures hiding behind a cropping of trees. It was at that point when 3 Bigfoot stepped out, stunning Alex since she had never encountered any of these beings previously. Her brother had mentioned that they did exist, but she never believed the accounts. In fact, this group of Bigfoot had been researched by JC Johnson and others in his group for approximately an 8-year period. When Alex told her mother about the encounter, she referred to the Bigfoot as her 'hairy boys,' so their presence was well-known."*

Like many other reservation reports, Alex's account notes the creatures were massive in size. She describes the largest one being as tall as twelve feet and having dark brown hair. The two that accompanied it were pegged as being ten feet tall, and eight feet tall, respectively. Again, eyebrows may be raised at the extreme height claimed, yet the fact remains there are constant reports from the region describing beings of this size.

Alex's description of the creatures mentions they had faces that were mostly hairless with flat, narrow noses and wide foreheads. She further notes that as she sat on the four-wheeler, frozen in shock, the creatures seemed to interact with her dogs, one of them even reaching down to rub the ears of one of the animals.

This is a curious aspect to Alex's encounter since many people report their dogs being attacked or taken away by the hairy creatures, yet in the case of Alex and her family, there seems to be no concern for the safety of the dogs. The nonchalant response of Alex's mother is an example of the calm acceptance Navajos display regarding the creatures in general. While not all residents are happy about the presence of these beings, they do for the most part seem to accept it as part of the reality of life on the reservation.

I've investigated with members of the Crypto Four Corners organization myself, high up in the mountains of the Four Corners region on tribal land. The mountains are a favorite spot for native sheepherders who camp high up with the flocks during the summer months, but we chose a deserted region for our expedition. During a few days in the rugged landscape we experienced incidents of distant calls that couldn't be identified, and evidence that something had crept around the campsite at night. Over the time we were there, rocks were thrown at our campsite along with large branches and logs that came flying from across a distance, at times landing very close to team members.

JC Johnson and I observed a large, black, bipedal figure walking along a ridge in the distance. It stopped and stood behind a large tree for some time, appearing to watch us as much as we were watching it. After a period of this mutual observation the creature vanished over the ridge.

We were confident the figure wasn't human and JC and I judged the height at about nine feet.

Additionally our camp was set at such a location where we could monitor if anyone else made the trip up the hazardous, unimproved road. Tribal officers had reported to us at the beginning of our expedition that no one else was in the area, and in fact once we made it to the top of the mountain, heavy rains set in making a trek up the rocky route extremely difficult, if not impossible for a time. Even with our four wheel drive vehicles, the trip back down was rather precarious over rocks and flowing water.

Fig. 3-4: JC Johnson and David Weatherly in the woods of Arizona.
Credit: David Weatherly

The Arizona Howler

"Howlers" seem to be reported fairly often on reservation land.

Perhaps the landscape allows the sound to carry further, or perhaps residents just hear tales of similar creatures on different parts of the rez and use the same catchphrase.

So it was that another "howler" plagued a reservation town far away from Crownpoint, across the state line in Arizona. During the summer of 2013, members of the community of Tsaile reported strange animal vocalizations echoing through the night. Like the incidents in Crownpoint, locals were unnerved by the weird calls, and the disruptions led to talk of Bigfoot.

The morning after one long night of screams, locals discovered a lengthy trackway of large, barefoot prints. The tracks were visible due to heavy rain the night before. Area residents Johnny and Carol Willeto took the information to renowned Bigfoot researcher Cliff Barackman, who followed up on the evidence.

The trackway came out of Canyon del Muerto and led to the edge of Tsaile Lake. The prints went into the lake at one point and then came back out. Around the shoreline of the lake, where the tracks emerged, pieces of fish carcasses were discovered scattered about. At that point the path led north through the desert and along a shallow ditch that paralleled the road a hundred or so yards to the east. The trail was lost after it turned onto a gravel road that led to a forested area of the nearby mountain, but the evidence was impressive. In total the trackway was visible for close to two miles and whatever had made it was careful to choose its path, finding the best cover available.

According to the report on Cliff Barackman's website: *"Many people in the community saw the footprints, and there was very little doubt as to what left them. When one combines the previous night's frightening vocalizations (a common occurrence that summer), the size of the footprints, the distance between them, the dead fish on the lake shore, and the fact that the track maker was barefoot for over two miles of difficult, prickly, pokey walking, the only conclusion that can be arrived at is that a sasquatch made the prints. For the Navajos seeing these prints, there was no doubt. Soon after the discovery of the footprints, several people in the community observed sasquatches nearby, and their sounds continued to be heard periodically throughout the rest of the season."*

Barackman found the trackway particularly interesting since it was clear the creature making it took care to avoid, as much as possible, areas where it could be seen by humans. The section of track where the least cover was offered ran near a well-traveled dirt road, but the tracks stuck to the only cover offered, a ditch.

The tracks measured thirteen inches and castings were made by the Willetos. Barackman's website has a full slideshow of the casts and he entered the information into his official database of discovered tracks.

Sasquatch in the Chuska Mountains

The *Farmington Daily Times* has covered the topic of Bigfoot on the reservation a number of times. In an article dated Feb 4, 2012 the paper spoke with people in the community of Sanostee, an area many researchers continue to consider a hot zone for Bigfoot encounters. According to the article: *"All of the accounts are similar: a hulking, hairy figure is sighted standing or walking upright, leaving giant footprints in the earth and spooking animals and humans. Other reports tell more gruesome tales of slaughtered or missing livestock."*

As mentioned previously the loss of livestock is a common trait in Bigfoot reports from Navajo country. Perhaps it's due in part to the rural nature of the reservation and the fact so many people own sheep and other animals. With livestock being one of the main food sources for the native population, perhaps Bigfoot thinks the same way. In the same article from the *Times*, another man told his story of a personal encounter with the creature: *"Raymond Peter, of Sanostee, remembers the first time he encountered Bigfoot.*

A sheepherder, Peter was in the Chuska Mountains at about 5 p.m. on July 4, 2009.

"First my dog Stookie started to growl," Peter said through an interpreter. "I looked to where the dog was growling, Bigfoot didn't see me, but I saw Bigfoot." Gesturing with his tattered NYC baseball cap, Peter indicated the creature was 8 or 9 feet tall, gray in color and about a quarter of a mile away.

"I could smell him," he said. "He really stinks, like it doesn't take a shower."

The creature was walking among the trees, heading west, Peter said. His face was covered in "shaggy hair" and his legs were "big, like tree stumps."

After the creature left, Peter said he found giant footprints in the damp earth.

"I didn't have a gun," he said. "After I saw that, I didn't want to be there anymore."

The article also recounts a report from another area resident who had an encounter high in the mountains: *"Sanostee resident Jerry Lewis said he recently saw Bigfoot in the Chuskas when he took his horse and donkey into the mountains.*

"My animals froze and I saw the thing walk over the hill," Lewis said through an interpreter. "It was taller than 8 or 9 feet, taller than the bushes, upright and hairy."

Lewis observed holes punched into the ice in his livestock trough, holes that looked like they were made by a fist.

Seeing Bigfoot may not be a good thing, however, Lewis said. Navajo legend states that when such creatures start coming back, it's an indication that the end of the world is near.

"Things that are happening now are things we learned about," Lewis said. "Once people know how everything works, when there's nothing else to learn, some of these creatures start coming back.""

Lewis's statements about the legends surrounding encounters with Bigfoot and the belief they signal the end times are one of the many reasons the subject has long been a taboo topic among Navajos. Stories of these hairy creatures go far back in tribal history. Like most native tribes, Navajo history is an oral tradition, passed down through the generations through storytelling, ceremony and other traditions.

There are some among the tribe who believe Bigfoot is a creature based in the spiritual world, the providence of those who work in the spiritual realms, and that there are greater implications to the growing number of reported encounters.

But some physical evidence of the long standing belief in Bigfoot can be found. Carved into the bluffs north of Sanostee are etchings reminiscent of the giant, hairy creature. No written records exist to indicate when the pictures were carved or who created them, but locals are quick to point them out as further evidence of the existence of Bigfoot in the region. Tribal elders say the drawings have been there as long as they can remember.

The carvings themselves depict giant beings with large heads, oversized hands and large feet with six toes. Other carvings show only massive footprints, leading one to wonder if the natives also referred to the creature by the size of his step.

BFRO Expedition in the Chuska Mountains

The Bigfoot Field Researchers Organization (BFRO), the nation's largest organization devoted to the pursuit of the cryptid, has conducted field work in the mountains on the reservation.

In 2002, the organization sent a team into the Chuska Mountains to search for evidence and to investigate reported sightings of the creature. The expedition lasted five days, from October 9th through the 13th.

The Chuska Mountain range extends from just north of Gallup, New Mexico into the northeastern portion of Arizona where it becomes continuous with the Carrizo range. The two ranges nearly connect with the San Juan range of the Rocky Mountains in Colorado. At their southern end, the ranges connect with the highlands of east central Arizona known as the Mogollon Rim. This area of the Mogollon Rim itself is rife with Bigfoot reports, and in fact is probably the most active area for encounters in the state of Arizona. Tales of the mythical "Mogollon Monster" of this region are eerily similar to modern accounts of Sasquatch.

Researchers believe this long zone of mountains may serve as a migration corridor, allowing the creatures to move freely over the vast range in accordance with seasons and the availability of food sources.

There's a lot of purported Bigfoot activity around the Chuska Mountains making it a desirable spot to search for evidence. It's common to hear reports of wood knocks, rock clicking, vocalizations and other odd sounds often connected to Bigfoot activity. Portions of the mountains tower high over the Navajo nation in New Mexico and parts of Arizona. Covered in piñon and juniper, the mountains have a rich topsoil making it easier to find tracks from known—and unknown animals—and as a result reports of Sasquatch tracks in the Chuskas are frequent.

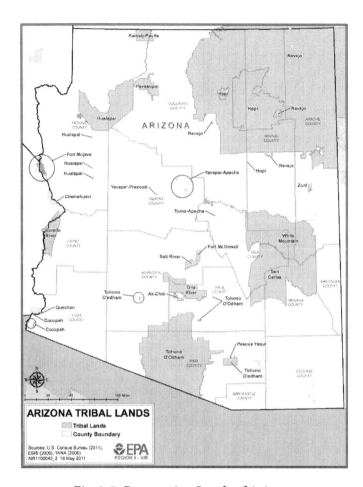

Fig. 3-5: Reservation Lands of Arizona

Team members Reid Nelson and Curt Nelson staked out an area they considered a hot zone for Sasquatch encounters. Reid, who works as an archeologist for the Navajo Nation has collected a lot of reports over the years, many of them from the Chuska Mountain range. His list of accounts includes reports from police officers, game wardens, ranchers and other residents of the region. Several of the incidents include observations of Sasquatch taking sheep and goats from local herds. In one incident, a local reported seeing one of the big hairy creatures kill a foal and take it away into the trees. In yet another reported case, a group of occupants inside a summer herding cabin were repeatedly harassed by a creature they described as Bigfoot.

The many summer camps high in the mountains may be providing a veritable buffet to any Bigfoot spending time in the area. Cattle and sheep on the reservation are free range, so they can graze over a wide swath of land. Since every animal cannot be monitored full time, there is ample opportunity for predators to avail themselves of the livestock. Perhaps Bigfoot sees the livestock as easy prey, and is taking advantage of the unguarded animals.

Fig. 3-6: C4C (Crypto Four Corners) member Tom Sirchia on the hunt.
Credit: David Weatherly

Fig. 3-7: Expedition Longview, Four Corners Region.
Credit: David Weatherly

Fig. 3-8: C4C Members Sirchia, Johnson and Weatherly.
Credit: David Weatherly

Conclusions

Native tribes all over the country have legends of giant, hairy creatures that dwell among us. If the old adage, "where there's smoke, there's fire," holds any truth at all, then it's important to consider, or perhaps reconsider these native tales and how they balance with modern reports of Bigfoot encounters. Native people knew about these creatures long before European settlers ever set foot in the Americas, and now thanks to a growing attitude of openness among some natives, they are speaking out about contemporary encounters.

The Navajo nation offers a unique set of dynamics in the study of Bigfoot. The large size of the reservation, combined with a small population spread out over the vast space, results in wide swaths of land with little or no human interference. This fact alone makes the area prime territory for unknown creatures to roam about freely. Add in the long history of Navajo lore surrounding these beings, the fact that many Navajos themselves are now investigating reports of these cryptids, and I suspect we will see a lot more information regarding Bigfoot coming out of the southwest.

Fig. 3-9: A Four Corners Morning.
Credit: David Weatherly

Hong Kong as a focal point for Bigfoot and Yeren studies

by Richard Muirhead

In this essay I will review the Chinese Wildman, known as the Yeren, by analysing events within the history of Hong Kong`s cryptozoology and beyond. In this way I will focus on certain aspects of the Yeren and in doing so focus to a more limited extent on North America`s Bigfoot. I am not attempting any overarching theme and if my approach seems rather scattered it is because I am attempting to connect various disparate elements within Hong Kong`s cryptozoology and mystery hominid studies.

By "focal point" I mean looking closely through sources such as old, English language, Hong Kong newspapers and journals, websites, library archives and resident memories I have managed to find. I will closely examine and continue to accumulate a very large body of cryptozoological and Fortean zoological information, including data and information on some mystery hominids. Wider lessons can be applied using this data to throw light on the Yeren and Bigfoot. Even in the early 21st century, Hong Kong could be described as an almost magical, very Fortean place, with its strange juxtaposition of former British colonial and Chinese influences. It has long been a borderline place, between East and West, Communism and Capitalism, occult and orthodox spirituality, and tropical and temperate fauna. Until the 1980s the border at Shenzhen was highly porous, with animals able to cross over largely unobserved.

There is a popular fallacy within cryptozoology that every cryptid is a `prehistoric survivor` that has somehow avoided discovery, and which lurks somewhere in the wilder areas of the globe. This is simply not true, and based on two completely fallacious principals.

1. Evolution somehow stopped when we reached the modern era.

2. The fauna of a specific biotope is static until somehow the

predations of humankind wear it down.[1]

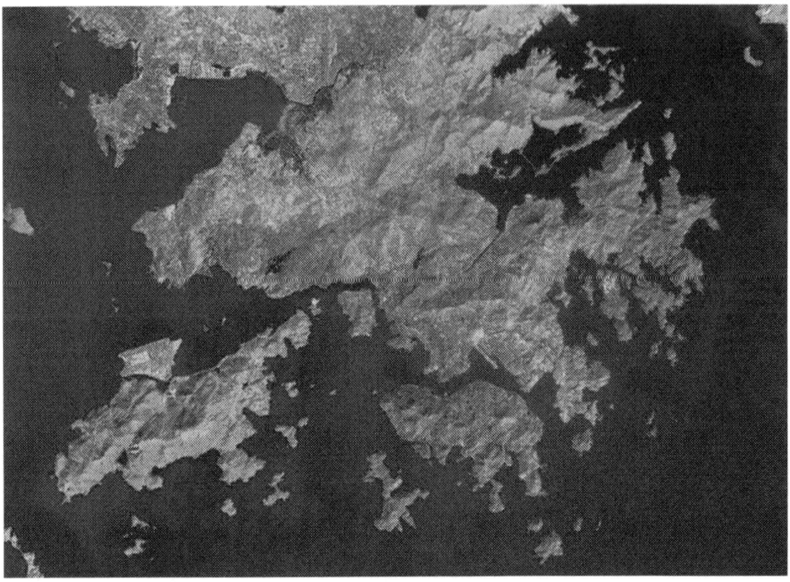

Fig. 4-1:Satellite Image of Hong Kong Region.
Credit: Googlemaps

The phenomena of Bigfoot and the Yeren are as much about human *perception of what these creatures are as to what they* actually are in reality. Take for example this image of two martial arts practitioners in China, reproduced with permission from the Taiping Institute. The photo was taken in the 1930s by the French photographer Louis-Philippe-Messelier. The name of this posture in martial arts is significantly for the purpose of this essay; namely the Monkey Fist but at first glance, outside of its context, it appears to show two adult men with learning difficulties or mental illness, almost feral, grimacing at each other, being stared at by a curious group of onlookers. What this image shows is long before the era of Photoshop or other technologies that can create whatever the photographer *wants* the viewer to see and believe, it was possible for one scene to be reinterpreted as something else. This has surely happened with regards to Bigfoot and the Yeren many times.

---

1   Jonathan Downes. The changing face of the species list of British Lepidoptera. Animals and Men issue 53 p. 56.

Fig. 4-2: Boxers Performing on the Streets of Shanghai, 1930.
Credit: Chinese Martial Studies, wordpress.com

An example of such a misrepresentation follows: On December 26th 1994 The U.K newspaper `The Daily Mail` reported under the headline `Bigfoot and the Chinamen` a story of a supposed Chinese Wildman, who actually was a tragic sufferer of a microcephalic condition (what an insensitive person would call a `pin-head`) but who the journalist Bob Chisholm passed off as a Wildman. To quote :"Deep in the Shennongjia mountain range of central China, I was sent to track down a half-man, half-ape creature said to provide the missing link in man`s evolution from the apes. It was never going to be an easy task to find him judging by the elusiveness of Wild Man`s cousins: the Abominable Snowman of the Himalayas and the

American Bigfoot."[2] Later Chisholm reported: "I asked Hu if he could give me any information about the story of the son of Wild Man. This was a local rumour that there lives in the mountains the offspring of a Wild Man and a shy human mother, who has moved to a secluded location where she can look after her grown-up but vulnerable son in peace and privacy, safe from the intrusion of scientists and journalists. Hu said he didn't have any first-hand information about this, but he did have some material in his museum. He fetched a video cassette, slipped it into his player and there, as clear as day, was Son of Wild Man. Son of Wild Man smiled. The smile was undoubtedly human but his sloping forehead and high-set ears were apelike. His hunched gait, as he clambered around a mountain slope munching a banana, also was ape-like, although he did not have the Wild Man's red fur...When I returned to Peking, a Western-trained doctor looked at the pictures and said: "This is a severely retarded human. He is microcephalic – this is a condition similar to cretinism and is often caused by inbreeding." Microcephalic means having a small brain, which also accounted for the sloping forehead and odd-looking ears. But why did the unfortunate young man walk like an ape and wear no clothes? "He was probably brought up like an animal," said the doctor. "People with such low intelligence are hard to train to behave like normal people."[3]

What we really have here is a non-story from a supposedly intelligent newspaper that should have known better, though to give it a little bit of credit they did acknowledge the Wild Man was nothing of the sort at all, but an unfortunate handicapped man being exploited for Western curiosity's sake. (A more interesting case was reported in an American newspaper of the early Twentieth Century, tainted with the racist assumptions of the time:

New Species of Monkeys

Strange Race Discovered in Island of Java Thought to Be Long-Looked for Missing Link

"The natives of that part of the island have long known the presence of...apes, which they call "Ash Petrizi". Unlike any other apes,

---

2   *The Daily Mail* December 26th 1994 p. 18.

3   Ibid p.19.

they bathe frequently and the females wear strange necklaces of twigs and red berries, and nurse their young singing half-articulated words. They have, in fact a language, but it consists of very few words."

Of course it is important to read reports like this in the context of the time but it also shows the racist aspects of evolutionary thinking and ignorance of aboriginal culture.)

But returning to China: "Readers of popular science magazines in the postMao era… gained much exposure to marginal subjects in foreign science, for example UFOs, lake monsters, Bigfoot, and the Guinness Book of Records. Popular science magazines, books, and film in the late 1970s and 1980s teemed with accounts of extrasensory perception and images of people with interesting deformities, such as extra limbs or thick hair all over their bodies. In this context, the hairy people…born with unusual amounts of body hair (who had appeared regularly in materials on human evolution since the republican era) became more explicit as sensational symbols of the freakish mysteries of nature, despite scientists` efforts to treat them as rational evidence of human evolution from apes."[4]

It needs to be remembered that believing in the Yeren or Bigfoot is similar to a "faith" experience in that some of us are certain it exists but we cannot see it or experience it. This isn`t blind faith, because we are basing our beliefs on an intelligent analysis of the data at our disposal. *As far as I know* the Minnesota Ice man is one of the very few cases of a cadaver being seen, photographed and examined to any extent, and when it was lost "Bernard Heuvelmans never recovered from the disappointment."[5]

Sightings of mystery animals, particularly Bigfoot and the Yeren are very much a matter of what the eyewitness sees or perceives as well as what actually *is* being seen. The Patterson-Gimlin film of October 1967 apparently showing a Bigfoot-like creature walking through Bluff creek, California is still being debated 47 years later, because of different *perceptions* of whether it was a person in an ape suit or a mystery hominid. Perhaps this is why there are so many Chinese hill creatures.

---

4   Sigrid Schmalzer The People`s Peking Man - Popular Science and Human Identity in Twentieth-Century China (Chicago: University of Chicago Press 2008) pp. 188-189.

5   Professor Bryan Sykes, lecture at College Oxford May 21st 2015

Due to the fact the Yeren, Bigfoot and many other cryptids are talked about in books, journals and the Internet to a massive extent, yet hardly ever revealed in verifiable and *undeniable* hard evidence, a whole air of "unreality" or "fantasy" attends those reports that reach the cryptozoological and wider community. Yet from a Fortean's point of view, this was Charles Fort's whole ethos. He would be the first to admit he was an iconoclast. By which I mean he set out to challenge and if need be, demolish the prevailing scientific orthodoxy.

Fig. 4-3: Charles Fort
Credit: oddsalon.com

One website calls him an "irascible iconoclast"[6]

---

6   http://blather.net/blather/2007/05/charles_fort_grave_albany_new_york.html

"As a writer, iconoclast, and founder of modern study of anomalous phenomena, Fort was a brilliant man. Few men can rise from such humble beginnings as his, to such dizzying heights of greatness, and yet remain so unknown."[7]

Hong Kong has been a crucible or "Fortean zoology nexus" certainly since the beginning of the Twentieth Century, and almost as equally certainly since way back in Chinese pre-history. (The 7th Century A.D. T`ang Dynasty Chinese annals[8] and later *Materia Medica* are full of extraordinary and anomalous beasts with little or no effort made to distinguish between "flesh and blood" animals and supernatural hybrids.) Hong Kong has also been a place whose zoology has been seriously misunderstood or misinterpreted, and this despite the fact it has been familiar to Westerners since at least the early 19th century, As late as the 1910-1911 (11th edition) of the *Encyclopaedia Britannica* the fauna of the former British Colony was being given as: "The animals are few, comprising a land tortoise[9], the armadillo, a species of boa, several poisonous snakes and some woodcock." This is grossly inaccurate, especially considering by 1910 Hong Kong had already been under British rule and well explored for almost 70 years! The closest reptile to a giant tortoise I am aware of from this area was the one in the Canton Zoo that died at the incredible age of 1000 in June 1947, according to *The China Mail*:

Canton Loses Its Tortoise

"The "City of Rams" has lost its 1,000 year-old giant tortoise which died yesterday, according to Chinese press dispatches from Canton. The tortoise, originally from the Paracel Islands, was one of the main attractions in Canton`s Han Min Public Park..."[10]

But concerning mystery primates, long before the giant molar tooth which may have belonged to Gigantopithecus, according to the

---

7   http://www.oocities.org/ianjkidd/CHARLESFORT.doc

8   See for example Francis Schafer : The Vermillion Bird: T`ang Images of the South.

9   In fact according to Hong Kong government websites and mainstream natural history books there have never been land tortoises in Hong Kong, in the sense of those on the Galapagos Islands, although currently 11 species of turtles are recognised in Hong Kong, including 5 species of sea turtles. The Paracel Islands in the South China Sea may once have been inhabited by large tortoises. See Richard Muirhead `Unexpected Tortoises and Turtles of the World` BioFortean Notes volume 3 (Greenville:2013) pp.40,42.

10   *The China Mail* June 13th 1947.

German-Dutch palaeontologist Von Koenigswald, and discovered in a Hong Kong curios shop in 1935, (possibly from Guangxi Province originally) there was the case of *Macacus Sancti-johannis*, the pigtailed macaque. This was named by Swinhoe in 1867 and was at that time an inhabitant of scattered islands to the south of Hong Kong, such as the Lema Islands which never fell under British rule. In 1870 he described the local monkey as *Macacus Sancti-johannis* and wrote: "This rock monkey is found in most of the small islands about Hong Kong and is like a Rhesus with a very short tail." He continued: "Dried bodies of this animal split in two are often exhibited from the ceiling in druggists shops in Canton and Hong Kong; and its bones are used for medicinal purposes..." According to Muirhead (i.e. myself) and Jonathan Downes: "It is disappointing to discover *Macacus-Sancti-johannis* is not distinct at a species level, but the mystery still remains. If this subspecies is different enough from the Rhesus Monkey to be accorded sub-species status, and if the tail is so short Sketchley claimed it was "pigtailed", then what actually happened to the Hong Kong populations?...It seems likely the genes which produce this "pigtail" are hidden somewhere within the gene pool of the Rhesus monkeys on Hong Kong Island itself. It also seems probable these genetic differences may yet assert themselves once more, and the zoologists of the future should be prepared to echo the words of Sketchley in 1893, and assert Hong Kong Island is the home to a distinctive pigtailed monkey!"[11]

Rare or little known species of monkeys still turn up today which gives encouragement to those cryptozoologists who believe Bigfoot or the Yeren is an unknown, very large, monkey-like animal. "Amazing images taken mainly by camera trips reveal a previously unrecognized species of macaque living in Tibet's forests. The photographs provide an intimate portrait of the cute primates – showing the monkeys grooming each other; foraging and tending to their young. The elusive monkey, which researchers have called the white-cheeked macaque (*Macaca leucogenys*) had previously been identified as the Assamese macaque (*Macaca assamensis*). But now researchers in China who took the images say the charismatic creature is a species in its own right.[12]

This pig-tailed macaque could be the candidate for at least one

---

11   The Mystery Animals of Hong Kong. Jonathan Downes and Richard Muirhead. The Anomalist no. 6. (Charlottesville: Spring 1998.)

12   Anon. New Macaque. *Want Tibet? Animals and Men* issue 53 May 2015 p. 13.

fairly recent Chinese Wild Man case. According to the *Fortean Times* in summer 1985 – `Wildman Rumour`: "On 23 October 1984, a small, hairy man-like (creature, beast?) attacked two young women with sand and stones in southern Hunan`s rugged Chengdu county in China. The women, one of them called Deng Yucui, 30, wearing a red jacket, fled home, and the following day 32 peasants from Shuitou village with 11 hunting dogs tracked down and netted the creature in neighbouring Xining county, which is honeycombed with caves. It clawed the ear off one human captor and was knocked unconscious with a pole. After a few days the "mao gong" or "hairy male" became used to his captors and started eating fruit and nuts. The peasants sold him to local traders for about £12, and he was exhibited in several cities, netting about £30 a day, and attracting the attention of scientists. He was confiscated by a county magistrate and handed over to the Wildman Research Institute, who put him up in a nice warm flat in Wuhan, capital city of Hubei province.

The story broke in the outside world after a report in the *Shenzhen Special Economic Zone Daily* in early February, which claimed that the 53 pound, 3 foot 8 inches tall creature was a yeti or a Wildman. Li Guangyu of the Wildman Institute described the beast as "having brown hair all over his body, with a big beard covering a face similar to a man`s. "He said the creature could eat and drink like a human and produced human-like sounds.

The initial excitement…was tempered by the short stature of the beast, and an article in the *Yangcheng Evening News* (9 Feb) finally put the dampers on. The front-page story quoted Li Jian, 62, deputy secretary of the Wildman Institute, as saying that the beast was a short-tailed rhesus monkey, though twice the usual weight, and with a tail 1½ inches long, half the usual length. He was middle-aged, about 15 years old. "He doesn't move around much. He`s pretty silent," said Li. "But when some girls walk in front of him he likes to get near them. He makes goo-goo eyes at them and says 'ah, ah, ah.'"[13]

"There are early references to the presence of strange primates [in China]. Two thousand years ago, during the Warring States period, Qu Yuan (340-278 B.C.), the statesman poet of Chu, referred in his verse

---

13   Anonymous. Wildman Rumours. *Fortean Times* no. 44. Summer 1985. p.13.

to "mountain ogres".[14] Another author states: "The misleading name on these maps is clearly a piece of up-to-date rationalism, which is encountered everywhere in this age. The modern Chinese, like many other races, say, that they don`t believe in `superstition` or `old wives' tales`. Everybody knows, of course, that there are no Hsing Hsing apes in China. They don`t exist, never did exist, they are pure mythology, inherited with so much other rubbish from the unenlightened and unscientific past. That is their attitude..." Science today does not admit the presence of the ape species anywhere in China."[15]

The Naturalist`s Pocket Magazine (1799) volume 3 mentioned great black apes of Maysi in China.

A report on *The New York Times* website on June 5th 1984, `On The Trail Of The `Wild Man` of China,` commented on the experience of a school teacher Mr Li in the early 1980s. He lived near the China-Burma border: "Mr. Li also displayed a thin, reddish strand of hair four inches long, one of a number that he said were collected, often snagged in tree bark, in Hubei, Sichuan, Hunan and Guizhou provinces. Most witnesses describe the wild man as having matted red hair, although black and white hair has also been reported."[16]

Janet and Colin Bord make the point: "Big Hairy Monsters seem often to take a particular interest in women (the Nowata, Oklahoma, BHM of July 1974, "bypassed houses where only men resided" and showed "a certain peculiar interest in women"), especially menstruating women; babies and young children; and courting couples." May these attractions perhaps have something to do with the person`s hormone output? In the instances cited (except perhaps for babies and young children), the people would be likely to be giving off strong hormone signals."[17]

There is even a suggestion Bigfoot has kidnapped Native

---

14   Myra Shackley *Yeti, Sasquatch and the Neanderthal Enigma* (New York: Thames and Hudson Inc 1986) p.79

15   Odette Tscher *In Pursuit of the Abominable Snowman* (New York: Taplinger Publishing Co) pp. 83-84

16   Christopher S.Wren `On the trail of the `Wild Man of China`. *New York Times* June 5th 1984 http://www.nytimes.com/1984/06/05/science/on-the-trail-of-the-wild-man-of-china.html

17   Janet and Colin Bord *Alien Animals* (London: Granada Publishing Ltd,1980) pp. 182-183 citing Clarke and Coleman *Creatures of the Outer Edge* and Stan Gordon `UFOs, in Relation to Creature Sightings in Pennsylvania,` paper presented to the MUFON UFO Symposium 1974, pp. 144-5.

American women based upon anecdotal evidence, such as amongst the Mono Lake Paiute Indian women giving testimony of being raped, and characteristic anatomical features, such as long fingers when compared to their palms, and an unusual amount of chest and arm hair. "One person seems to have hair that resembles a different color other than black, perhaps reddish."[18] The woman who was raped by the Bigfoot had a son who was hairy with a big head. At first he was rejected but later accepted as he was a very good hunter who "had uncanny natural abilities of sight and smell and was very strong... Many of his descendants are now scattered in many of the Paiute tribes in California and Nevada."[19]

The Nephilim, the giants of the Bible, were said to be the offspring of fallen angels and human women. Genesis chapter 6 verse 4, American Standard Version: "The Nephilim were in the earth in those days, and also after that, when the sons of God came unto the daughters of men, and they bare children to them: the same were the mighty men that were of old, the men of renown."[20] Perhaps these encounters involved kidnapping and rape?

In June 2015 I posted the question "Please can anyone tell me what they think of stories of Bigfoot kidnapping and mating with humans?" on the American Primate Exploration/A.P.E. Facebook group and I received the following replies. I am keeping the respondents names anonymous.

J.B. "Serpentine Long was abducted by a mama and baby Bigfoot and held for a year. The Sasquatch put pitch on her eyelids so she couldn't see where she was. Somehow she finally escaped. I don't believe they mated with her..."

M.L. "Dogs can adopt kittens.

I doubt that a human child would survive the outdoors exposure. Or the diet. I can - nearly - believe kids snatched for curiosity, then abandoned. Or eaten. If they exist."

D.B. "I find it extremely hard to believe. I've heard this before. There's no evidence of it to my knowledge and is purely speculation in

---

18   Bigfoot Evidence blog http://bigfootevidence.blogspot.co.uk/2012/12/did-sasquatch-kidnap-native-american.html

19   Ibid

20   American Standard Version of the Bible. Genesis chapter 6 verse 4

my opinion."

M.T. "Indian tribes have stated their women have been taken by BF for years. Native American tribes around Oklahoma have stated their people were taken and eaten. Anything may be possible..."

J.K. "John W. Burns interviewed Serephine Long who claimed to have been abducted by a sasquatch. She mated with the sasquatch while in captivity. The night she was released, she gave birth to a child who died. There is also the story of a man named Patrick and his two sisters in Washington State who are thought to be Skanicum or human-sasquatch hybrids. They had huge jaws and sloping foreheads. Only DNA testing would prove whether they were hybrids. All three are dead and their burial places unknown."

D.B. "That's amazing John! I really didn't know that! Thank you!!!"

M.L. "Often the interbreeding of close species is because of behaviour and looks. Not genes. Take ligers.

The technical impossibility is not an issue because human male has the biggest penis of primates. Gorilla has a tiny one. Sasquatch..?"

D.R. "Know the Russians attempted the breeding of various apes with humans: http://io9.com/the-man-who-tried-to-make-human-ape..."

T.K. "It's been recorded that great apes have abducted human children, after their own babies have died. So it wouldn't surprise me if occasionally a male, or female Sasquatch were to abduct children to replace the ones they've lost. Missing 411, has a number of stories where people go missing in national parks. Some being found alive, dead, or not at all. Also some are missing all of their clothes. I've read, & also know of a case, where a sub adult bigfoot was pursuing a young girl. So, no it wouldn't surprise me if occasionally this is happening. Maybe that's why when they get the DNA results back that it's coming up human."

J.B. "Thank you JK... I wasn't sure if they mated or not... Interesting..."

T.K. "There was a story of a man who worked for the railroad, I want to say late 1800s to early 1900. That went missing while working. After a few months he made it back to town, only to tell of this wild story, that he was abducted by a female Bigfoot. He also had said, how she licked his feet raw with her tongue, so he could not escape. He died shortly after from internal injuries. Apparently the female Bigfoot tried to mate with him, & in doing so crushed his eternal organs."

Richard Muirhead. "Don't you mean INTERNAL organs? This side of heaven we don't know what our ETERNAL organs will be? If any!"

This was the basic substance of the whole discussion.

Does the Yeren kidnap people? In an online interview comparing Bigfoot and the Yeren, Joshua Blu Buhs, author of 'Bigfoot The Life and Times of a Legend' and Sigrid Schmalzer, author of 'The People's Peking Man: Popular Science and Human Identity in Twentieth-Century China', Blu Buhs says "There are parallel stories about kidnapping, marauding wildmen."[21]

The late anomaly collector William Corliss, who died in July 2011 stated: "If the Yeren are only an undescribed ape, no anomaly exists. Our anomaly rating, however, is based on the possibility that the Yeren are hominids."[22] He also stated: "A wide spectrum of evidence hints that a large, hairy hominid prowls the mountainous, thickly forested region around Shennongjia, in Hubei Province, China. It is from this region that hundreds of contacts with this creature have originated. Other provinces, too, in central and southern China, seem to be host to this animal that the Chinese call the "Yeren", which translates as "wildman". The quality of these reports, however, is generally low; because *the country folk often apply the term Yeren to well-known primates prevalent in the region* (emphasis my own) and even to the relatively large, hairy Western cryptozoologists who invade their country looking for the Yeren!"[23]

Corliss later cites F.E. Poirier and J. R. Greenwell who specifically state (and this is pertinent to the 1984 case above and any similar);" There is no tail."[24] Yet opinion seems divided on the point about the tail, as one website mentions a case in 1957 when a wildman was killed in Zhejiang Province, but this turned out to be a macaque. Another candidate is the endangered golden monkey.

---

21   Chinese Wildman. http://www.bigfootencounters.com/creatures/wildman.htm

22   W. Corliss *Biological Anomalies: Humans III* (Glen Arm:1994).p.142

23   Ibid. p. 143

24   Ibid. p. 143

Corliss classified the Yeren as Anomaly Evaluation Level 1, stating: "If the Yeren are only an undescribed ape, no anomaly exists. Our anomaly rating, however, is based on the possibility that the Yeren are hominids."[25]

A whole atmosphere of fantasy surrounds the Yeren to a much greater extent than Bigfoot. Indeed there are as many as 14 different types of Chinese hill-monsters. As follows: Damaoren, Feifei, Fufu, Fujian Apes, Jue, Jueyuan, Kui, Maoren, Muke, Ruren, Shan Gui, Xiao, Xiaoyang, Xingxing.[26] Many of the Chinese ape-men/women seem to have supernatural abilities, just as Bigfoot is reputed to have in places such as Pennsylvania with connections to UFO sightings.

The very scarce booklet Wild Man China`s Yeti *Fortean Times* Occasional Paper Number 1.`by Yuan Zhenxin and Huang Wanpo with Fan Jingquan and Zhou Xinyan contains in an Appendix the following `Brief Bestiary of Chinese-Hill Monsters`: The Damaoren was also known as `Big Hairy Man`. Feifei wore their hair dishevelled, were good runners and ate men. Another commentary said they had long lips, a black hairy body and their heels were at the front, living in the mountains of Guangdong, Guangsi and Jiangsi Provinces. "The *Er Ya* written by Luo Yuan, 12th Century A.D. says: when the Feifei catches a man, it laughs for joy, folding its upper lip over its head, and then devours him. So men wear bamboo tubes on their forearms and, when seized, draw out their hands and nail the beast`s lip to its forehead, letting it run around blindly until it dies."[27]

The FuFu were literally, beings with "disheveled hair, a common trait of most of our anthropoid monsters."[28]

Fujian Apes: This is an account of how soon after the establishment of the Qing dynasty (1644-1911 A.D.) a monk found some wounded apes in a forest who had been attacked by wolves. The apes were cared for by the monks and later helped defend the monastery against an attack by Qing dynasty troops.

The Jue were supposedly a kind of ape. De Groot translates `Jue`

---

25   William R. Corliss op cit p. 142.

26   Yuan Zhenxin and Huang Wanpo. Wild Man China`s Yeti. *Fortean Times* Occasional Paper Number 1. (London:1981) A Brief Bestiary of Chinese Hill-Monsters pp. 19-21

27   J J M De Groot *The Religious System of China Volume 2*, Leiden, 1892-1910 pp. 507-509.

28   Yuan Zhenxin and Huang Wanpo. *Wild Man China`s Yeti* op cit p.19.

as `certain large gibbons` and gives a passage from the *Shu Yi Chi* (by Ren Fang, 460-508 AD): "Monkeys, when 500 years old, change into Jue attaining the age of 1,000 years, then become old men." It was a common belief in old China that animals gained transcendent powers and the ability to take on human form when they attained a supernaturally advanced age, such as a thousand years. This notion applied as much to mundane animals such as the fox and tiger, as to hill monsters."[29]

Jueyuan: "They waylay female travelers and kidnap the beauties among them, distinguishing the women by their smell, and never abducting males. Having captured a `wife`, the Jueyuan builds a house for her. Should she not bear a son, she stays with her captor for good, and after 10 years her shape becomes like his, and she no longer thinks of home. If she has a child, she is sent home immediately. The child always has a human shape, and when grown is not unlike ordinary men. Mothers who decide not to raise the child usually die."[30]

Kui: This word has been translated as dragon or walrus. "However the *Shuo Wen* also gives [a definition] as `a greedy quadruped, generally stated to be a she-monkey resembling a man`...They had a human face and an ape-like body, and were able to speak."[31]

Maoren: "A `Hairy Man.` Used generally for mystery anthropoids. This is also the usual modern Chinese term for atavistic humans born with a full coat of hair."[32]

Muke: "Guests of the woods...The term might equally be taken as `strangers in the woods.`"[33]

Ruren: "A `Like-a-man.` "Liu Yiqing (403-444 AD) says in his *You Ming Lu*, that beings `resembling men`(*Ruren*) live in Shandong Province, (N.E. China) 4-5 *chi* in height (1.32 metres), going naked with disheveled hair 5 or 6 *cun* long (16.5-19.8 cms). They utter screaming and whistling cries and, unseen, fling stones. They roast frogs and crabs for food." (De Groot, Book 2, p.509)

Shan Gui: "A demon or ghost of the hills and mountains, or

---

29   Yuan and Huang op cit p. 20

30   Yuan and Huang op cit p. 20

31   Yuan and Huang op cit p. 20

32   Yuan and Huang op cit p. 20

33   Yuan and Huang op cit p. 21

mountain-demons collectively. All the `species` mentioned in this bestiary could be classified as differing forms of Shan gui."

Xiao: "The term is applied very generally to the mountain-monsters. According to the *Shen Yi Jing* (attributed to Dong Fangshuo of the 1st C. BC, but probably 4th or 5th C. AD), xiao are human beings living deep in the western mountains, more than one *zhang* tall (3.3 metres). They go naked and capture frogs and crabs, occasionally accosting travelers in order to roast their food at the fire, or to steal salt. They can be scared off with fire-crackers, but when attacked give their assailants fever. They are also called *xao*, and can take other forms." (De Groot, Book 2, p.500)

According to a Bigfoot website: "The sasquatch is an omnivore with a substantial carnivorous component to its diet. They have been observed directly to eat leaves, berries, fruits, roots, aquatic plants and other vegetable matter, catch fish, dig up clams or ground squirrels, and prey on poultry, deer, elk and bear. In addition, they eat other odd items, such as young evergreen shoots, crayfish, road kill, meat or fish from human storage sites, hunter-killed game animals (these sometimes snatched in front of the hunter), and occasional garbage. They take an occasional livestock animal, but not with sufficient frequency as to produce organized persecution.

They appear to kill large prey animals by a blow with the fist, rock or stick or by twisting their victim's necks, sometimes to the point of decapitation. Liver and other internal organs are their first targets. The remaining meat is sometimes stored on the ground under a haphazard shelter of sticks or lifted into tree forks above ground. No compelling evidence exists that they store food in any substantial way beyond this; only rarely has a sasquatch been observed carrying a fish some distance from its origin, or a deer, presumably into hiding."[34]

Xiaoyang: "Literally means an `owl-goat`, but Hawkes (David Hawkes: *Ch`u Tz`u. The Songs of the South.* Oxford University Press. 1959 p. 139.) gives it as an anthropoid monster inhabiting wild places, whose upper lip covers its face when it laughs."

Xingxing. "According to the *Shan Hai Jing* (E.D. Edwards: *The Dragon Book*. Wm Hodge & Co. 1938 p.144) the Xingxing are like

[34]   Bigfoot Field Researchers Organization Frequently Asked Questions http://www. bfro.net/gdb/show_FAQ.asp?id=586

monkeys with white faces and pointed ears, walking upright like men and able to climb trees…Tchernine (Odette Tchernine: *The Yeti*. Neville Spearman. 1970. pp 86-87.) … and goes on to quote a story from the *Peking Daily* of 29 January 1958 that a Chinese film director, Bai Xin, working with the PLA in the Pamir mountains in western Xinjiang, encountered `wildmen` in 1954. On the first occasion, he and his colleagues saw two short `men` with backs hunched, climbing a nearby slope. They shouted and fired some shots in the air, but the `men` continued climbing and disappeared among the rocks. On another occasion, Bai and a photographer followed large footprints for 1½ km, and found some traces of blood, before darkness forced them to give up the pursuit. And on a third occasion, near Mount Muztagh Ata in the Pamirs, Bai was staying with some frontier guards who threw out some meat thought to be tainted. During the night, the guards reported seeing a `wildman` in the bright moonlight, apparently wrapped in white fur, pick up the meat and run off with it. In modern usage, the name Xingxing is applied to the orangutan."

There was a case of a suspected orangutan reported in the *North China Herald* of June 11th 1886 (page 10) from Canton: "An animal called a *jén hsiung* (manbear), probably meant for an orangutang, is said to have been met on the banks of the West River, between this place and Hsun Chou Fu, in Kuang-si. This animal is said to fly at the appearance of living human beings, but to delight in the desecration of graves, and devouring of the dead. This is probably meant to be a malicious satire on the American Missionaries, who have been trying to establish themselves in Kuang-si, and are said to have extended their scientific researches to the mortal remains of several of the natives. A tall American or other missionary with a bushy ill-kept beard , would be enough to give a Chinaman the idea of a human bear or man-bear, *jén-hsiung*; and prowling about amongst the graves looking for native skulls or jawbones would suffice to give ground for declaring the strange animal to be a desecrator of graves."[35] This gives a very interesting sociological twist and insight into the politics of the time.

According to Myra Shackley, mystery hominid expert, "One can propose the following hypotheses to account for China`s Yeti:

    1.   Everything is invented and these creatures do not exist.

---

35   *North China Herald* June 11th 1886 p.10.

2. These creatures DO exist and are either a previously unknown or a previously unclassified variety of primate.

3. Other possibilities, such as 'throwbacks' to primitive types, men who have literally 'gone wild', hermits/idiots living in wild places.[36]

Option 3 above includes the Cheung Chau, Hong Kong's 'feral man' which was reported on the Hong Kong history website gwulo. com. Even in the mid-1980s Cheung Chau was a rural backwater which was best known in folklore circles for its annual festival involving people climbing a tower of buns and its fishing villages. On September 5th 2013 Tung posted on gwulo.com: "The long-eared wild man we saw, around 1953-54, was half-naked, perching on the bushland bordered between this hidden valley and the CLCY village. He was also seen covered with fur skin and leafy clothing with weird hair decorations from seashells, eyes so red like being on fire and voice very low-pitched, as a very old man. He was big, more hairy than normal, kind-looking and quite majestic, like a Chief from the Amazon forest. His ears were very big, long and curled up with hairy tips on each top. He smoked with a very long bamboo pipe and seemed always on guard on his tiny territory with a rod like a prophet under the torching sun, sometimes eagles and ravens flying in circle in the sky above. More than once he wanted us to come closer to his den which was like an opening to some unknown shelter next to this forest. For the sake of our parental advice, we never accept his plea, our curiosity always directs our thinking that he might be a fairy because his location was on the edge of the area known as Sen Yan Jiang which means 'The Fairy's Well.'" Tung.[37]

Of course every continent has experienced its own feral people, whether they be children raised by animals or humans who have chosen to "go native".

The case of the Shanghai ape-man is one of the few cases of an urban or suburban wild man – globally. *The China Mail* of August 26th 1947 said: "Reports of the Pootung monster spread to Soochow Creek and families living in sampans were made panicky and confused during the night by stories of a half-human, half animal monster that scratched the eyes of several children living in sampans. The reports started last

---

36   M. Shackley op cit pp 87-88

37   Gwulo.com September 5th 2013. http://gwulo.com/atom/15615#comment-25602

week in the Pootung area and spread quickly up and down the water front. The reports, coupled with rumours that an abduction gang is in operation, led to six volunteer policemen beating a woman to death in an attempt to get a confession and beating another unconscious..."[38] I have found an urban Bigfoot case dated from 1921. Any others before or after this date are very scarce. A report, dated July 30th 1930, from the Elyria, Ohio, *Chronicle Telegram*, runs thus:

Report Ape Seen Near Sandusky

Homeville, Ohio, July 30 – "The elusive ape that has left a trail of terror in towns between Sandusky and Norwalk was reported to have entered a dwelling here today and frightened John Rucker and his wife from their home. Mrs Rucker was first to see the animal entering the house by a rear door. As she screamed, her husband sighted the ape and grabbing his wife by the hand, fled from the house. Sheriff John Parker of Sandusky was called , but deputies failed to find the animal. Instructions have been issued by the sheriff to capture the animal if found."[39]

In Hong Kong a story emerged several years ago from the British Columbia Scientific Cryptozoology Club of a wild-man kept in a cage by a wealthy Chinese man in Kowloon in the 1960s. The website said: "An anonymous informant of the BCSCC recalls that as a child growing up in Hong Kong, he had unusual neighbours who kept a strange animal in a cage which filled an entire room of their house. The wealthy neighbours were kindly in their own peculiar way and took immense pride in showing our informant the bizarre freak of nature called a Yiren – also variously spelt as Yeren, Yeh Ren and Yen Hsiung (man bear). Our informant says that he had only a morsel of courage to take more than a fleeting look at the strange creature as it sat in a corner of its cage. It appeared to be jet-black in colour and had a very oddly-shaped conical head. From what our informant could make out of the beast it looked like some sort of fantastic ape."

The witness is not alone. All over Asia villagers in remote areas have reported a strange animal that walks upright and appears to

---

38   Muirhead`s Mysteries: An Ape-Man in Pre-Communist Shanghai/Chinese Forteana. *Cryptozoology Online* October 26th 2010.

39   Chad Arment *The Historical Bigfoot* (Landisville: Coachwhip Publications 2006) p. 245

be the product of hybridization between man and ape. As ghastly as the prospect of such a union is to most people it seems more than likely that there is a species of bipedal ape wandering Asia that is seen as more mischievous than malevolent. From past gleanings researchers have deduced that there are two types of wildman lurking in the bush: the gigantic dark-furred ape-like beast closely resembling Gigantopithecus; and the shorter reddish-brown furred animal which walks upright, but looks more like a monkey.

There appear to be a proliferation of sightings from China hence our decision to classify the animal – at least temporarily – as the Chinese Wildman or Yiren as it is known in Chinese. Although it is readily apparent that there are two types of wildman only, local nicknames have meant that there are sometimes as many as five different types to be considered, but from local descriptions we can eliminate at least three of the types as known apes and monkeys.

In some cases eyewitnesses have described an animal that sounds remarkably like the Orangutan, but they were adamant that what they had seen was not that particular member of the pongid family. The creatures described did not always walk upright and were observed to have dropped to a quadruped stance on a number of occasions making identification even more difficult. Some have posited the possibility of the Golden monkey as the real culprit, but once again witnesses have dispelled this notion by saying they could tell a golden monkey from a Yiren.

During the 1950s and 60s, Hong Kong movie makers used the Yiren as a sometimes benevolent —and at other times malevolent— part of the fabric of Chinese folklore. Several films depict the Yiren as a rather dense animal quick to change allegiances when resoundingly taught a lesson in the fighting arts by some handsome hero of southern Chinese folklore. Our red-brown friend usually behaved as if it were a pet after its subjugation by the hero. Not the case with the larger black variety, which required the services of a particularly gigantic Hong Kong actor known as the Frankenstein of Asia. The black monster which went by the name Xing Xing or Sing Sing in Cantonese – was a nasty piece of business whose destruction would culminate into its evaporation complete with some really awful rudimentary hand drawn special effects explosions.[40]

40   Yiren/Chinese Wildman http://www.bcscc.ca/blog/?p=70

The orangutan is certainly a good candidate for the Yeren. Gregory Forth in his 'Images of the Wildman in South-East Asia' said: "An interest of a different kind is the selection of 'hsing-hsing' by modern Chinese zoologists as the vernacular name for the orangutan... Also positing a large primate, Greenwell and Poirier suggest that the representation may reflect a remnant population of orangutans or a related species of *Pongo*."[41]

Wikipedia says: "The two orangutan species are the only extant members of the sub-family Ponginae. This subfamily also included the extinct genera *Lufengpithecus*, which lived in southern China and Thailand 2–8 million years ago (mya), and *Sivapithecus*, which lived in India and Pakistan from 12.5 mya until 8.5 mya."[42]

I also uncovered another Hong Kong wild-man report from the 1940s which was originally posted on the Hong Kong history forum gwulo.com: "There were bands of large apes reported in the Tai Tam area in a book from the 1940s. A friends' campsite was approached by one in the 60s and they fled pretty quickly. Not the same species as the monkeys out near Shing Mun, but larger and darker...I (Richard Muirhead) came across a Chinese website mentioning a kind of black-haired ape man or spirit-being near Aberdeen on the south side of Hong Kong Island."[43]

The iconography of the Wild Man is universal in geographical space. There is an image on the web of the Yeren from a poster in China circa 1997, depicting all the characteristic traits of the iconic creature: broad shoulders, lengthy fur framing an ape-like face, a solid trunk over imposing limbs, with its right hand raised to the sky, as if in greeting. I also own a statue of the Wild Man (I call it Johnny Wildman) that makes me think of what the Yowie, the Australian mystery hominid, might look like. I bought it at an antiques shop in England but the shop owner had no idea where it came from. It is important to try and interpret what these two separate depictions convey. The Yeren in the Chinese poster gesticulates in what can be perceived as a friendly manner, the right arm raised in greeting, its left arm laid placidly across its stomach. In reality, the Yeren is either

---

41   Gregory Forth. *Images of the Wildman in South-East Asia* (2008) pp 194-195.

42   Wikipedia. Orangutan. https://en.wikipedia.org/wiki/Orangutan

43   Muirhead's Mysteries: Some New Hong Kong Cryptozoological Oddities. *Cryptozoology Online*. November 19th 2013

very shy or quite aggressive. My furry, Yowie-like "manimal" statue passively stands holding a stick which reaches up to its chest, perhaps revealing a discrepancy with cryptozoological eye-witness accounts. The Yeren and the Yowie may be shy — but not passive. They have been known to avoid human company but they are hardly ever known to stand passively by doing nothing as Homo sapiens might.

Seeing as this essay has been concentrating on the stranger aspects of mystery hominids, I thought I`d end with one of the strangest reports of all, about a white Yowie, from the Brisbane, Queensland `Worker` of June 26th 1909:

Wild Man of the Woods

"During the Past Few Weeks residents between Mudgee and Hargraves, New South Wales, have been disturbed from their slumbers by strange noises. These remained a mystery till one afternoon last week. At about 5 o`clock they were again heard, and several persons residing in the locality were astonished to see a peculiar animal, about 5ft high, standing on his two legs, and brushing away, with his claw-like hands, long unkempt looking hair from his eyes. The animal was covered with long white hair, and when seen was uttering cries similar to those which have been disturbing the peace of the neighbourhood. The hairy man, or whatever he is, was only seen for a minute, and disappeared as suddenly as he came."[44]

---

44   The Worker June 26th 1909.

.

Is Bigfoot a Giant Form of Homo erectus?

by Ken Gerhard

In innumerable cultures worldwide there exist accounts of hair-covered, 'wild men' who dwell deep in the forests. While to some degree these beings come in different shapes and sizes, for the most part they are described as being powerfully built and gigantic in stature, as well as displaying physical characteristics between both ape and man. For those of us who are receptive to such ideas the crux of the debate has always been – Provided they actually do exist, taxonomically which family do they belong in? Are they merely pongids, great lumbering apes that have evolved with an exclusively upright gait? Or perchance are they hominins, early sub-humans that retain archaic traits such as excessive hairiness and muscle mass? As humans, this particular distinction is important to us for very profound reasons. The answer could potentially reveal clues about our own origins and true nature.

For about six decades now, the most popular theory has revolved around an immense fossil anthropoid known as *Gigantopithecus*, which is known from hundreds of truly enormous fossilized teeth, as well as four mandibles that have been discovered in China, Vietnam and India beginning in 1934. Based on theoretical reconstructions it has been estimated that 'Giganto' may have stood ten feet tall and weighed over half a ton. While its genus currently resides in the subfamily that includes orangutans, it is unclear whether *Gigantopithecus* was a knuckle walker or moved around on two legs, since no bones from below the neck have been found. It's a given such a massive primate would by design have lived a terrestrial rather than arboreal existence. Based on studies of its dentition, it would appear Giganto's diet consisted primarily of vast amounts of bamboo, grasses and other vegetable matter. These creatures lived alongside human precursors including *Homo erectus* during the late Pleistocene, hundreds of thousands of years ago, and probably left an indelible impression on our kin.

When we consider *Gigantopithecus* fossils have been found in regions where there traditionally have been reports of cryptid wild men – The Yeti of the Himalayas, the Yeren of China and the Nguoi Rung of Vietnam, a potential connection seems intriguing. Furthermore, it's not impossible to envision an extant population of these impressive anthropoids could have migrated over the Beringia land bridge that once connected Asia to North America during the last glacial period, thus explaining legends and sightings of Bigfoot or Sasquatch, as well. The great heights that are often associated with these so-called monsters (reputedly towering over humans), is significant since we know of no other primates that achieved such a stature. Nevertheless in light of recent discoveries, as well as other factors, perhaps it's time to consider the possibility that a widespread and highly adaptable human ancestor might instead be responsible for accounts of our man beasts. If relict hominins have truly managed to remain undetected in the remote wilderness areas of our planet, they may very well represent an excessively robust form of *Homo erectus*.

Scientists speculate *Homo erectus* (known popularly as Java/Peking man) evolved in Africa around 1.8 million years ago and spread out into Asia, Oceania and Europe (*Homo heidelbergensis*) for the next million years or so. Some have even mused that *erectus* may have reached Australia at some point. Incidentally, The Land Down Under boasts its own mythical man beast known as the Yowie. A relatively recent excavation suggests one potential and diminutive subspecies (*Homo floresiensis*) remained extant in Indonesia as recently as 12,000 years ago. During 1996 a research team working along Java's Solo River uncovered some *H. erectus* fossils that were initially dated as recent as 35,000 to 50,000 years old, indicating they might have coexisted with later humans. A contemporary reassessment concluded the fossils were at least 143,000 years old, which is roughly about the time when most scientists think *erectus* became extinct. Regardless, based on its impressive longevity and distribution in the fossil record, *Homo erectus* was easily the most successful hominin form ever. Now, it must be recognized that anthropologists express a great deal of disagreement over how to properly categorize most pre-human fossils, so there is really nothing definitive that can be said about any of them. Paleontologist Lee Hales puts things in perspective. "The problem is that we are rarely dealing with a complete skeleton, not to mention that we can't be sure what stage of development we are looking at in a particular species. Essentially without all the information it winds up being a matter of pure speculation." And yet based on the available data it would appear some *H. erectus* offshoots might have displayed both remarkable adaptability and physical diversity, including robust types that may have conceivably approached Bigfoot-sized dimensions.

In 1941, the influential German/Dutch paleontologist Ralph von Koenigswald (who incidentally had also found the very first *Gigantopithecus* tooth) was excavating the Sangiran archeological site on the Indonesian island of Java. This has turned out to be one of the most fertile locations in terms of harvesting *Homo erectus* fossils. Von Koenigswald subsequently unearthed the mandible of a hominin that appeared far greater in size than any specimen dug up before. Shortly before being captured and ultimately imprisoned by the Japanese army, he made a duplicate plaster cast of his find and sent it off to a colleague in Germany for identification. Finally during 1945, physical anthropologist Franz Weidenreich announced his conclusion – In his opinion, the mandible seemed to represent an enormous hominin that may have stood up to eight feet tall. Weidenreich tentatively named the species *Meganthropus paleojavanicus* (Large man from ancient Java). Since that time, a handful of possibly related jaws and skull fragments have also been discovered, though debate regarding both the validity and phylogeny of the entire lot rages on.

Dr. Karl P.N. Shuker is one of the world's leading cryptozoologists and possesses a PhD in comparative physiology. He has this to say. "*Meganthropus* is a very mixed bag of fossil evidence, so much so that it has generated all manner of extreme, implausible notions, especially ones indicating that this was a giant form. With no post-cranial remains available as far as I'm aware, estimates of height based on jaw and teeth dimensions are very risky and have not been formally accepted in peer-reviewed literature. Indeed, as yet there is no consensus as to where *Meganthropus* fits within the hominid lineage, or whether the genus is valid." Still, some anthropologists continue to speculate Von Koenigswald's giant mandible may represent *H. erectus*, although apparently outside of its generally accepted size range.

So what is the generally accepted size range of *Homo erectus*? In 1984 the most complete skeletal remains of an early hominin ever unearthed were dug up in East Africa by a team led by noted anthropologist Richard Leakey. Dubbed 'Turkana Boy' it is believed the being was around eight years old at the time of his death, though he already stood five feet, three inches tall. Thus it's not unreasonable to assume a full grown, Turkana Man would have stood over six feet, taller than the average *Homo sapiens*. According to professor Lee Burger of South Africa's University of Witwatersand, "One of the most interesting things that the fossil record reveals is that we went through a period of extreme gigantism." One *Homo heidelbergensis* femur Burger analyzed belonged to an individual who would have, in his estimation stood seven feet tall.

Despite its manlike posture, *H. erectus* was very different from us, possessing a heavy brow ridge, rapidly receding forehead and smallish skull that limited the size of its cerebral cortex. In fact all of his cerebral lobes were smaller than in *Homo sapiens*, with a total brain capacity between 900 to 1100 cubic centimeters. Though we cannot be sure, estimates suggest his intelligence may have been about 60% of an average human. That said, there are indications that *H. erectus* was resourceful at times, potentially utilizing fire and fashioning stone tools, figurine-like artifacts and even primitive rafts used to travel short distances over water. Compared to modern humans he was powerfully built. It is unknown if he was excessively hairy, but being active in the warm, open grasslands of the mid Pleistocene would not have necessitated it.

A key element to consider when attempting to link *Homo erectus* to our cryptid wild men accounts, is the fact many eyewitnesses who have had face to face encounters with these beings remark that their faces do look surprisingly humanlike. It's also worth noting many Native cultures have for centuries viewed beings like Sasquatch as essentially giant men, often depicting them as a primitive, savage tribe that chooses to live in the deep wilderness. Moreover, it stands to reason that the fact they've managed to remain so elusive implies our man-beasts must possess some degree of strategic awareness. Virtually all of the great apes had been catalogued by the early 20th Century, as they did not have the wherewithal to avoid detection by humans. Apes are by nature very loud, demonstrative, impactful and smelly animals that noticeably impact their environment. They are not known to be all that stealthy.

The obvious problem with the *Homo erectus* hypothesis is the fact despite thousands of documented reports, there is no indication Bigfoot-like creatures are advanced enough to wield fire or fashion tools. Personally, I think it is conceivable the abstention of fire usage by these beings would be a desirable adaptation, if they were attempting to avoid being tracked and hunted by *Homo sapiens*. An opportunistic omnivore that stands seven feet tall and weighs several hundred pounds would qualify as an apex predator (at the top of the food chain) and thus have no need for fire as a defensive asset. Additionally, in the vast wilderness there would be many food sources available that would not require cooking. If (as the accounts indicate) our wild men are covered all over by long hair, then they would not require fire for warmth.

With regard to Paleolithic tools, it's true such implements have never been found in conjunction with Bigfoot. However many investigators, including myself, have come across intricate, tee pee-like structures and other unnatural branch formations that seem to have intelligence behind them. Bigfoot researcher Richard Noll claimed he once found an elk bone that had been embedded in the carcass of another animal, apparently used like an axe. Similarly, a mutilated deer carcass found near Canyon Lake, Texas in 2015 had a bloody, sharp edged stone lying under its carcass. An October, 1953 account from Casey County, Kentucky describes a Bigfoot that was observed using a piece of firewood like a hammer.

Fig. 5-1: Bigfoot Spear Fishing. Is it possible that Bigfoot occasionally uses tools or weapons?
Credit: RobRoy Menzies

It has been conjectured Bigfoot creatures may bury their own dead. This is highly speculative of course, but would certainly explain why no one has ever stumbled upon a carcass. We could reasonably view such behavior as a human trait, a ceremonial act. During September of 2015, anthropologists officially described a new species of archaic hominin called *Homo nedali*. A mother lode of its fossilized bones were discovered deep in a South African cave, and it appears as though the remains had been placed there intentionally. The age of the remains has not yet been determined, but based on their physical features preliminary estimates put them at one to two and a half million years old. It's therefore reasonable to assume that *H. erectus* may have hidden their dead in a similar fashion.

Interestingly, there exist audio recordings of alleged Bigfoot vocalizations analyzed by at least one expert linguist who has determined them to represent a rudimentary language. Known as the 'Sierra Sounds' the bizarre noises were recorded in California's Sierra Nevada Mountains by Bigfoot researchers Al Berry and Ron Morehead during the early 1970s. In recent years a former military linguistics expert named R. Scott Nelson of Missouri took an interest in the recordings and undertook an extensive analysis of them. Summarily, Nelson feels the vocalizations represent a sort of archaic dialect, uttered using primitive vocal chords. Bearing this out, alleged Bigfoot abductee Albert Ostman claimed he was once kidnapped by a family of Sasquatches at the head of British Columbia's Toba Inlet while on a prospecting trip in 1924. Ostman later stated that while he was being held captive, the alpha male of the clan shouted a warning to him using what sounded like a word – 'sooka.' Now, while we certainly must acknowledge great apes such as chimpanzees and gorillas seem to display impressive communication skills at times, true language – spoken words— are considered to be one of the defining markers of men. Regarding *Homo erectus*, a 2003 scientific paper from India concluded, "The development of its speech centre, would have been started but the supralarygeal (vocal apparatus) never adapted for a complete speech process." Based on endocasts of its cranial vault, the Broca's area of the *H. erectus* brain indicates it could have processed a type of language. A rudimentary but incomplete attempt at speech seems like a fair description of the Sierra Sounds.

At this juncture it might be useful to compare alleged descriptions of Bigfoot-like creatures to *Homo erectus* in order to gauge whether there are physical similarities. Obviously there is no photographic evidence of a Sasquatch that is considered to be conclusive. But, perhaps the closest thing we have to a bona fide snapshot is the so-called Patterson Film, which was captured at Bluff Creek, California on October 20th, 1967 by a pair of intrepid investigators. Most readers are familiar with this controversial piece of footage and I will spare an in-depth analysis of its pros and cons for another time, though suffice it to say in four-plus decades the authenticity of the film has never been disproven... nor adequately duplicated by modern Hollywood special effects experts who have attempted it. This remains the iconic image of a Bigfoot. Unfortunately, due to the poor quality of the resolution (the subject was a good distance from the photographer and walking away swiftly as the photographer was in the act of stumbling toward the subject, resulting in shaky camera work) the facial features are indistinct. Reconstructions of its features based on one famous frame where the creature turns to look back at the photographer, seem to show a strikingly human-like face. Its bulbous, hooded nose with downward facing nostrils is quite apparent. Apes tend to have scant, upturned noses with forward facing nostrils. Digital computer enhancements have reinforced the notion that in profile the subject in the Patterson film displays a fairly flat (orthognathic) face corresponding to that of a hominin, with no evidence of sub-nasal prognathism as displayed by apes.

Fig. 5-2: Recreation of the head and face
of the subject in the Patterson Film.
Credit: RobRoy Menzies

One of the most celebrated observations of a Sasquatch occurred on British Columbia's Mica Mountain during October of 1955, involving a professional hunter and trapper named William Roe. Because the specimen moved very near to Roe's position without noticing him, the expert outdoorsman was able to obtain a detailed look at its features for several minutes. He later stated in a sworn affidavit. "I leveled my rifle. The creature was still walking rapidly away, again turning its head to look in my direction. I lowered the rifle. Although I have called the creature 'it,' I felt now that it was a human being and I knew I would never forgive myself if I killed it." A similar scenario played out in The Dalles, Oregon in the early evening on June 2nd, 1971. High school music teacher Richard Brown was returning home when he spotted what appeared to be a Bigfoot standing in a nearby field. He ran inside his home and grabbed his rifle, ultimately studying the beast through an 8x scope for a good five minutes at a distance of about 150 yards. At one point he began to pull back the trigger, yet discovered he wasn't able to shoot the thing. Brown later recalled, "It looked more human than animal." The files of Bigfoot researchers are brimming with similar declarations. Evidently, those few people who have managed to end up in close proximity to these beings have remarked about how human looking they appear. Pennsylvania's so-called 'Incident at Narrows Creek' involved an alleged face-to-face encounter by investigator Ken Storch who later enlisted a forensic sketch artist to reconstruct what he had seen. The resulting image remains one of the most human-looking Bigfoot personifications one could hope to imagine.

Skeptics like to point out there seems to be an inordinately high degree of variation in terms of Bigfoot descriptions, one example being hair color. Witnesses have mentioned black, dark brown, light brown or blonde, auburn and even a silver or white pelage. Sometimes the head hair is said to hang down to the shoulders, while other times it is said to be uniform with the body, about two inches long. While the body of Bigfoot is generally characterized as stocky and muscular, claims of surprisingly slender Sasquatches emerge from time to time. To what do we owe these discrepancies? If we work under the assumption we are dealing with nothing more than a species of undiscovered ape, then this would be unexpected. However, a wider degree of variation might make sense if these beings were wide-ranging hominins. Merely consider the three or four races that comprise the species *Homo sapiens*, not to mention the highly unique traits we each display as individuals.

Some of the most compelling evidence with regard to Sasquatch is the cumulative miles of gigantic humanlike footprints found and often photographed or cast with plaster. Their morphology remains surprisingly consistent, displaying a superficial resemblance to human feet though much larger and broader, possessing a longer heel and noticeably lacking an arch. Physical anthropologists including the late Dr. Grover Krantz, as well as his colleague Dr. Jeffrey Meldrum have noted the relevance of such features, as they would make perfect sense for a bipedal primate that weighed several hundred pounds and spent much of its time trekking up and down mountains. Of utmost significance is the fact the hallux or big toe is perfectly adducted (aligned) with the other toes, like in hominins, and not divergent as is always the case with apes. Dr. Meldrum, who has spent years studying Bigfoot tracks in depth, once remarked during a lecture that the archetypical Sasquatch track reminded him of fossilized *Homo erectus* prints discovered at the Terra Amata site in southern France.

Because anthropologists possess a wealth of *Homo erectus* fossils, most feel they are able to theoretically reconstruct a reasonably thorough model of the hominin's physical and behavioral characteristics. That said, the process called evolution does occur, and if descendants of *erectus* are still around, they've had plenty of time to undergo dramatic changes that would have aided with their adaptation and survival into modern times. The real question is – Would the potential benefits have even warranted such a transformation? I've already suggested the possibility the species may have chosen a more rudimentary existence, regressing in terms of its technological development. While this doesn't seem to make a lot of sense on the surface, if competition with *Homo sapiens* drove them into remote wilderness areas, they may have adapted a more primitive and nomadic lifestyle in order to avoid direct competition with us. Additionally, dramatic morphological changes may have occurred, which made such a transition palatable.

The Last Glacial Period of the lower Pleistocene epoch began roughly 110,000 years ago and lasted until 10,000 to 12,000 years ago. Known as the true Ice Age, it was a time when large portions of the planet were covered with expansive glaciers. The climate worldwide was frigid, to say the least, and many animals grew to enormous proportions, since the conditions favored creatures whose greater mass enabled them to retain heat more efficiently. This was the era of massive megafauna – wondrous woolly mammoths and rhinos, mastodons, beavers the size of bears, bears larger than any known today and towering Irish elk with antlers a dozen feet across. In the Americas, giant ground sloths like Megatherium were as big as modern elephants and armadillo-like glyptodonts were the size of cars. Whose, to say a gigantic form of hominin descended from robust *erectus* stock might not have sprung up around this time as well? Would such a giant not have benefited in its daily struggle against these mighty megafauna animals? Again quoting a 2003 scientific paper from India, "There were undoubtedly several subspecies of *Homo erectus* in different geographical zones and they would have doubtless differed in ecology and behavior." A perfect example is tiny island-dwelling *Homo floresiensis*, nicknamed 'the hobbit' because it only stood a paltry three and a half feet tall; essentially the complete opposite of our theoretical giant *Homo* strain.

The excessive hairiness described with regard to Bigfoot and its cousins can also be explained as an adaptation to a rapidly cooling planet. I've already addressed the fact anthropologists speculate savanna-dwelling groups of *H. erectus* probably lacked excessive body hair, but we can't possibly know for sure. Regardless, there were woolly proboscideans (elephants) and rhinos during the Ice Age, why not excessively hairy hominins? One could hardly hope to argue against the benefits of inhabiting an arctic landscape while brandishing an extra layer for warmth. Most evidence of Bigfoot, the Yeti and others still seems to be concentrated in mountainous areas of high elevation where the advantage of such a pelage would be apparent.

Provided our hypothetical giant, hairy, brutish *Homo erectus* offshoot did arise elsewhere, there is another obstacle to overcome when attempting to link it to Bigfoot, since no remains of *erectus* (or any other archaic hominin for that matter) have ever been confirmed in the New World. However, during 2002 it was announced a Mexican anthropologist named Federico Solorzanzo made an intriguing find while sifting through boxes of bone fragments he had collected from the shores of Lake Chapala, in the western state of Michoacan. There was one fragment that seemed to correspond perfectly with the cranial brow ridge of a *Homo erectus* skull. Because the item seems so utterly out of context, most scientists reject it out of hand. Not withstanding, there have been controversial stone tools found in South America estimated by some to be almost 50,000 years old; roughly 36,500 years before the first humans are believed to have migrated to the Americas from Asia.

Eventually, new discoveries will no doubt push back the antiquity of hominins in many parts of the world. Fossils are, after all, extremely random and hard to find treasures that require very specific conditions in order to be preserved for countless eons. Accordingly, science books are constantly being re-written as new fossils are unearthed. Truth be told, there remain enormous gaps in our fossil history, while our family tree appears to be more like a tangled bush.

Ultimately, while it is tempting to choose a conclusive identity for our enigmatic wild men, it remains imperative that physical remains of Bigfoot (or one of his many cousins around the world) be found and examined by qualified experts in order to determine their true nature and classification. To the majority of the population this will never happen, since most people view the monstrous man beast as merely a legend, perpetuated by the fertile imaginations of those who feel the need to fill their lives with a sense of mystery and wonder, or somehow connect with our primordial past. There is an intriguing theory that our ape-men merely represent a distant memory of interactions between *Homo sapiens* and early hominins, a collective remembrance passed down for tens of thousands of years, or perhaps even imprinted in our DNA. Yet in light of mounting evidence, it is becoming difficult to not at least consider the possibility these beings could conceivably exist. Dr. Jeff Meldrum has astutely pointed out multiple types of hominins coexisted on our planet for millions of years. Why should present day be the exception to this rule? There are two key points that must be considered – Our world, while seemingly becoming smaller due to rapid advancements in communication and technology, still boasts vast expanses of uninhabited and even unexplored habitat. This paradigm is reinforced by the fact science books are constantly being rewritten as remarkable new animals are still being discovered on a regular basis… and sometimes, new men as well.

On August 29th, 1911, a desperate Native American man named Ishi walked timidly out of the dense brush near Oroville, California. The last surviving member of the Yahi tribe, presumed to be long extinct, Ishi had been living unnoticed on the fringe of civilization for over forty years, and interestingly within an area which produces a substantial number of Bigfoot reports. The isolated Korowai people of Papua New Guinea were living at a stone-age level when they were first encountered by western scientists on March 17th, 1974. And as recently as 2011, a primitive, jungle dwelling tribe known as the Mashco-piro emerged from Manu National Park in southeastern Peru. These Natives have had virtually no contact with civilized people through the centuries and have maintained the same way of life for thousands of years. Such occurrences bode well when considering the possibility of a small but viable population of *Homo erectus* descendants remaining similarly hidden... deep in the remote and inaccessible wilderness areas of our planet.

Fig. 5-3: Recreation of a Sasquatch kidnapping
prospector Albert Ostman in 1924
Credit: RobRoy Menzies

ORANG-PENDEK:
on the Track of Sumatra's
'Short Man'

by Richard Freeman

From the earliest age I suffered from that wonderful malady men call 'wanderlust'. Growing up with thrilling and exotic images of distant lands and strange creatures from magical series like *The World About Us* and *Life on Earth*, I would always be dissatisfied with suburban, industrial England. Add to the mix an early addiction to Jon Pertwee's *Doctor Who*, then is it any wonder I became a cryptozoologist?

My work has taken me to every continent save Antarctica. I have searched for the Tasmanian wolf, the Mongolian death worm, the yeti, the giant anaconda, the almasty and many other creatures, but it is Sumatra and its 'short man' that keep calling me back.

Orang-pendek means 'short man' in Indonesian. The creature is said to be powerfully built and immensely strong, but relatively short at around 3 to 5 feet in height. It walks upright like a man and rarely, if ever, moves on all fours. It is generally said to have dark brown, grey or black fur, but honey-coloured or reddish hair has been reported. Sometimes a long mane of hair that falls down to the shoulders is also mentioned.

The orang-pendek generally seems to be a solitary creature, though there are rare reports of groups of them being seen together.

Many Indonesians fear the orang-pendek on account of its massive strength, but it is not thought of as aggressive. Often the creature will move away from any human it sees. It is said to occasionally use rocks and sticks as crude weapons, hurling them when it feels threatened. Like most wild animals it is probable the orang-pendek might become aggressive if cornered or surprised.

Its diet is primarily herbivorous, consisting of fruits, vegetables and tubers. There are some reports of the animal ripping open logs to get at insect larvae. Rare reports tell of it taking fish and freshwater molluscs. Early reports tell of some of them feeding off the flesh of dead rhinoceros that had fallen into native pit traps.

Native knowledge of the creature goes back into the mists of history, and there are a number of localized names for the orang-pendek around the Island. It is called sedapa or sedapak in the south-eastern lowlands. Gugu is the name in southern Sumatra, whilst in the Rawas district it is atu rimbu. In Bengkulu it is known as sebaba.

One of the earliest accounts comes from William Marsden in his 1784 book, 'The History of Sumatra: containing an account of the government, laws, customs and manners of the native inhabitants, with a description of the natural productions, and a relation of the ancient political state of that island.'

William Marsden (1754-1836) was an English orientalist who joined the East India Company at the age of 16 and was sent to Sumatra, where he became principal secretary (presumably a liaison) to the Dutch Colonial government. In his book he mentions a race of wildmen covered in long hair and rarely met with.

There are many instances of encounters with the orang-pendek during the Dutch Colonial period, and in particular the first few decades of the 20th century. During this time much was written about it. Interest waned in the 1930s, and apart from a chapter dedicated to the orang-pendek in Bernard Huevelmans' book 'On the Track of Unknown Animals,' the creature was almost forgotten.

As Indonesia opened up as a tourist destination in the 1980s new reports began to come in. They were consistent and sometimes made by highly reliable people. There is not the space here to leg the legion of sightings, but a fairly comprehensive list may be found in my book 'Orang-pendek: Sumatra's Forgotten Ape.'

Instead, here I will concentrate on my own experiences and my own thoughts on the animal.

I first ventured into the rainforests of Sumatra in June 2003. The small expedition team consisted of Dr. Chris Clark, Jon Hare and myself. We contacted Debbie Martyr, a travel writer turned conservationist. Debbie, who now resided in West Sumatra, had become the head of the Indonesian tiger conservation group. She has seen the orang-pendek on more than one occasion. Debbie was very helpful, suggesting where to look and what guides to employ.

Whilst in a hotel in Padang, the unattractive capital of West Sumatra, we met a man in his fifties (called Stephano) who claimed to have seen orang-pendek. He told us in 1971 he had accompanied an Australian explorer called John Thompson into the jungles of Kerinci-Seblat national park. He had seen small human-like primates with yellow hair. In order to stop Thompson shooting them he told the Australian a curse would descend on anyone who killed one of the creatures.

Sadly before we could question him more our transport arrived to convey us south to Sungai Penuh were Debbie Martyr lived.

The next day we met Debbie Martyr. Debbie is a charming lady who reminded me a lot of the chimp conservationist Jane Goodall. A former journalist, Debbie first came to Sumatra as a travel writer in 1993. She had heard tell of orang-pendek and assumed it was a legend, no more than a bit of local colour. Later a guide was telling her of the animals he had seen in the jungle. He said he had seen rhino, sunbear, tiger, elephant and orang-pendek! About six weeks later Debbie herself saw the animal.

Debbie told us the most recent sighting, about 3 months previously, had taken place in the jungle surrounding Gunung Tuju, or the Lake of Seven Peaks, a large volcanic lake in the park. She photocopied several maps for us and also spoke of a lost valley. Despite being shown on the map, Debbie told us no one had ever been there. It looked like a couple of days hike from the lake, and the contours showed a wickedly steep-sided canyon.

We all felt it would be exciting to look for the valley, and Debbie arranged for guides to lead us in. Sahar was a small bespectacled man in his early thirties, who, if dressed in a suit and tie could pass for an accountant, along with his brother John and an older man called Anhur.

We travelled down to Sahar's village, Polempek, and next day began the expedition proper.

Fully stocked, the six of us set out into the foothills of Gunung Tuju. The foothills were fine but as the gradient grew more acute I began to suffer. Gunung Tuju is 3000 meters high. Much of the way the path is at something like 75 degrees. Imagine a gargantuan winding staircase, with stairs made of moss-slick tree roots jutting at differing angles. Like the labour of Sisyphus in Greek mythology, the climb seemed never ending. I collapsed with exhaustion, staggered on, collapsed again and vomited with overexertion.

Finally we made the summit. The land falls away dramatically to the 4 km lake, Gunung Tuju, a strange, unearthly turquoise in colour. It lies in the bowl of an extinct (or maybe just dormant) volcano. The lake's waters are biologically impoverished, and geothermal influences keep it warm. Only one species of small fish and one species of freshwater crab live there, but nevertheless support several fishermen who sometimes come up from the village.

Using fishermen's canoes so decrepit they could have come off the Ark we crossed the lake. Whilst the others set up camp, Sahar led Jon, Chris and I out into the jungle. Sahar`s skill as a guide was astounding. The slightest bent twig or misplaced leaf caught his eye. Things you or I would walk straight past tell him the secrets of the jungle. He pointed out the trail of a Malayan tapir (*Tapirus indicus*) through the bushes, where the bulky animal had hardly disturbed the greenery, yet later we found its three-toed footprints.

We came upon a possible orang-pendek footprint unfortunately damaged by rain. I measured the print but it was too damp for casting. It was narrower at the heel than at the front, and pressed about half an inch into the ground. Further along the trail we came across seven prints crossing a large muddy puddle. Similar in size and shape to the earlier print they too had suffered rain damage. The gait was definably that of a biped. A fallen log crossed the puddle, and as Sahar pointed out, a human would have crossed by the log as opposed to walking through the mud.

A little further on Sahar indicated some damaged plants. Known as pahur, the pith inside the stem is a supposed favourite food of orang-pendek. A number of the plants seemed to have been dexterously peeled apart and the pith eaten. A flattened area of moss on a nearby tree stump may have been where the creature sat whilst eating. We hid and waited in silence, but apart from the calls of birds and insects nothing disturbed the stillness of the jungle.

Sahar told us that in 2000 he heard the cry of orang-pendek. He demonstrated....

"UHUUUUUUUUR-UR-UR" ....A weird, drawn out moan followed by two grunts. Quite unlike any animal vocalization I know.

In the 1980s Sahar`s father and a friend had been cutting logs to build a house close to where the village of Polompek now stands. The area has long since been deforested. Both men saw a bipedal ape lifting up cut logs and throwing them about. It was covered in blackish-brown hair and was about five feet tall. The hair on the creature's spine was darker. Its legs were short and its powerful arms were long. The face was broad and black in colour with some pink markings. Both men fled.

Each day Sahar took us out on jungle trails. We collected a number of hairs but did not come across any more footprints. Thus we spent the days of our first expedition and decided to leave the 'lost valley' until next year.

As we climbed down again we saw more wildlife in a single afternoon than in the whole of our stay at the lake. Mitred langurs (*Presbytis melalophus mitrata*), a banded linsang (*Prionodon linsang*), a normally nocturnal member of the civet family, a small toothed palm civet (*Arctogalidia trivirgata*) and a pair of horse tailed squirrels (*Sundasciurus hippurus*). We also found the droppings of a golden cat (*Catopuma temminckii*).

Back in Sungia Penuh I interviewed Debbie about her sightings.

Me: Could you please tell me how you first heard about and got interested in orang-pendek?

Debbie: I was travelling in Sumatra as a journalist in 1989. I was climbing Mount Kerinci and heard of a legendary animal that I thought would add a bit of colour to the travel piece I did. Then I started meeting people who claimed to have seen something that didn't appear to exist. At that stage I didn't believe or not believe, I was trained as a journalist, which is a respectable profession, so I took a look into it.

Me: Can you tell me about the first time you actually saw orang-pendek?

Debbie: I saw it in the middle of September; I had been out here four months. At that time I was 90 percent certain that there was something here, that it was not just traditional stories. I thought it would be an orang-utan and that it would move like an orang-utan, not bipedally like a man. I had my own preconception of what the animal would look like if I did see it. What was the real shocker was that I had been throwing away reports on the animal on the basis of colour that didn't fit into what I thought the animal would look like. When I saw it I saw an animal that didn't look like anything in any of the books I had read, films I had seen, or zoos I had seen. It did indeed walk rather like a person and that was a shock.

Me: What did it actually look like?

Debbie: A relatively small, immensely strong, non-human primate. But it was very gracile, that was the odd thing. So if you looked at the animal you might say that it resembled a siamang or an agile gibbon on steroids! It doesn't look like an orang-utan. Their proportions are very different. It is built like a boxer, with immense upper body strength. But why an animal with immense upper body strength should be lumbering around on the ground I don't know. It makes no sense at all.

It was a gorgeous colour, moving bipedally and trying to avoid being seen. I knew there was something in the vicinity because the action of birds and primates in the area meant that there was obviously something moving around. So I sent a guide around as far as I could to where the disturbance was. Whatever was concealed in the undergrowth would try to avoid my guide and move away in front of him. I was concealed looking down over a small shallow valley. We didn't know what we were going to see. It could have been a bear, it could have been a tiger, it could have been a golden cat, or anything. Instead, from totally the wrong direction, a bipedal, non-human primate walked down the path ahead. It was concentrating so hard on avoiding my guide it didn't look towards me. I had a camera in my hand at the time but I dropped it I was so shocked. It was something so new my mental synapses froze up for a minute trying to identify something I hadn't seen before.

Me: You have seen it a couple of times since. Could you tell me about those sightings?

Debbie: I saw it again about three weeks later. Again it was on Mount Tuju and again I had a camera in my hand, again I froze because I didn't know what I was seeing. It had frozen on the trail because it had heard us coming. All I could see was that something across the valley had changed. I looked through a pair of binoculars. Something didn't look quite right in the landscape. By the time I trained on the area the animal, whatever it was, had gone.

Those were the only times I could have got a photo of it. I have seen it since but fleetingly. Once you have seen an animal you can recognise it. If you have seen a rhino you can recognise a bit of a rhino.

Debbie also showed us a cast of an orang-pendek footprint taken a few years previously in the jungle surrounding the lake. It was about 8 inches long and did not resemble a yeti or Sasquatch footprint. It was much less human looking. It had four longish toes at the front and the big toe was placed further back along the side of the foot. The toes all looked more prehensile than a human's but less so than any known ape's.

Debbie also believes early Dutch explorers may have collected orang-pendek specimens without knowing what they were. Bones and skin from this cryptid may be languishing in the basements of Dutch museums mislabelled as orang-utan!

We then moved on to check out another sighting area.

After a backbreaking trek we reached a remote village called Sungi-Khuning. We stopped in a large (by village standards) house in the centre of the village. I was unsure whether it was a guesthouse, village hall, or just some hospitable soul's home. Sahar said a man who had recently seen orang-pendek lived in the village and would come to talk with us. That night about 23 people crowded into the house but the witness was not among them. Apparently the man was a poacher who had set a snare for deer. Upon checking it he found he had caught an orang-pendek. The powerfully built, five foot tall ape was struggling with the snare. The poacher tried to jab the orang-pendek with his spear but the beast smashed it to matchwood and screamed at him. At this point he fainted. When he awoke the creature had pulled itself free and was walking off into the jungle. It was hair covered, with long, powerful arms and walked erect. The man himself however was not in the village at the time. Excursions into the surrounding jungle provided no further clues.

Once we were back in England I sent hair samples off to my old friend Dr Lars Thomas of Copenhagen University for analysis. The team at Copenhagen headed by Dr Tom Gilbert specialize in retrieving DNA from old or damaged specimens. The samples all turned out to be from tapir or golden cat. However, I was convinced there was an unknown species of ape in West Sumatra and resolved to study the area again.

Several weeks later Debbie e-mailed me to say a honey-coloured orang-pendek had been recently reported from Renah Permatk. It had supposedly killed three dogs. The locals set out to catch it and Gunung Tuju was crawling with people armed with cameras. Needless to say nothing came of the hunt.

The same team returned to Sumatra in May of 2004. This expedition was to concentrate on the "lost valley" Debbie had told us of on our previous visit. Situated beyond Gunung Tuju, the mysterious region had never been penetrated by explorers.

We were to meet up with Mr Surbandi, the owner of a small rural hotel. We stayed with him briefly in 2003. He was a keen birdwatcher and naturalist and had found some orang-pendek witnesses for us to talk to. The witnesses lived less than an hours drive away in a village called Te Uik Air Putih. The village backed onto an area called "the garden," an area of cultivated land used for growing crops. The garden merges with the jungle seamlessly and in some areas is very overgrown. Due to its more open nature one usually encounters more wildlife in the garden than the jungle proper. By a remarkable stroke of luck a specimen of the titan arum (*Amorphophallus titanum*), the world's largest flower, was blooming in the same area. The flower blossoms only once in ten years so this was an un-missable opportunity.

The titan arum did not disappoint, and is truly the Godzilla of flowers, looking like some strange surrealist sculpture or something made by the BBC special effects department. It stood seven feet tall. The elephant's foot of a stem widens into a barrel-sized green bowl, which in turn flares out into the petals which look like nothing so much as a Spanish Flamenco dancer's red dress. Finally a phallic spadix of bright yellow rises from within the petal's folds.

We found the house of the witness and interviewed him via Mr. Subandi. His name was Seman, a middle-aged man with a young child. Seman witnessed the creature in an area of land adjacent to a river at mid-day in February 2004. Back then the area was overgrown and the creature was only visible from the waist upward. He estimated it to be 80cm tall, but when we looked at the area ourselves it seemed the animal must have been over a meter tall. The height he indicated with his hand appeared to be one meter as well.

The animal had short black hair, a broad chest with visible pink skin, long ears and a pointed head possibly indicating a sagittal crest. The creature vanished and Seman said he had the feeling it had fled to the river and swam across it, though he did not see this. The river was a torrent when we were there but in February it was much lower. Seman said the creature had been in view for approximately three minutes.

On visiting the area we determined the creature had been about 22 meters away from the witness. Seman produced a sketch showing a powerfully built, ape-like creature with broad shoulders, long arms, and a conical head. At no time did it raise up its arms, as gibbons are wont to do on the rare occasions they move about on the ground.

We returned to the same general area the next day to interview another witness. Ata was in his twenties and had seen his creature about three weeks after Seman. He heard a strange cry coming from the same area of the garden where Seman had his encounter. The noises began at 10 am, a loud OOOOHA! OOOOHA! sound. Upon investigation Ata found himself only five meters away from a strange beast. It was one meter tall and had short black hair with a prominent chest that made him think it was female. Its lower half was hidden by vegetation.

He noticed it had large owl-like eyes, a flat nose, and a large mouth. It seemed aggressive, and Ata said he felt the hairs on the back of his hands rise up in fear. He produced a drawing of a muscular, upright creature with large, round eyes, but it lacked the pointed head of Seman's description.

Next day Sahar, his brother and another guide arrived and we left for a remote village called Kutang Gajha. We spent two days lost. Sahar was not au-fait with this area. By pure chance we stopped by a farmhouse where the people there said one of their relatives, a man called Pak Suri, knew the way to the lost valley. Pak Suri was away that day and would not be back until the morning, so the family kindly put us up for the night.

It transpired that Pak Suri would not be returning the next day as at first thought, but another man Pak En, who also knew the way, was contacted. Pak En was a sprightly old man who had ventured into the valley years ago on a fishing trip and agreed to be our guide for the next few days.

Next day we set off beset by leeches, flies and biting ants, daubing our boots in damp tobacco to drive the leeches away.

Finally we came to the valley and discovered there was a damn good reason why it was named "lost." Sheer cliffs fell a thousand feet into rapids and the sides of the valley were swathed in savagely-thorned rattan. We had no rope. If we wanted to see the bottom of the valley we would have to risk scrambling down by hand.

Pak En found a part of the valley wall slightly less than perpendicular and we gingerly began our descent. What looked like solid ground would often be no more than a loose topsoil of leaves and would cascade from underfoot. Sturdy looking branches would be rotten to the core and snap whilst being used for support. Half sliding, half walking we made our way precariously towards the bottom.

Walking out into the sunshine of the valley, it was astounding to think I was the first Westerner ever to set foot in this mysterious place. It was more of a river-carved gorge than a valley, with the fast-flowing river dominating the area. The waters were tough, though not deep or very wide, but quite fast with scattered, slippery rocks for a bed. The only place large enough to build our camp was in a small area of jungle close to where we had descended. A bit unnerving since the river looked as if it could flood violently and quickly.

At camp that night Pak En told us he had seen an orang-pendek in the jungle just above the valley three years ago. He was walking along a jungle trail when he saw it approaching. It was one meter tall, upright, and powerfully built. It had black hair with red tips and a broad mouth with prominent breasts that made Pak En think it was likely a female. He noticed it grasped the vegetation as it moved and let out an OOOOHA! OOOOHA! sound. He watched it move down the trail for two minutes before it saw him, then quickly turned about and walked back the way it had come from. Pak En's tale that night was eerily lit up by thousands of green fireflies throughout the camp.

The next morning after breakfast Sahar, Jon, Chris, Pak En, John and myself set out to explore the valley. The landscape compelled us to keep crossing the rapids on foot. The banks would peter out into sheer cliffs on one side forcing us to cross to the other. Some areas of the cliff faces were stripped clean by landslides, where hundreds of tons of earth, rocks, and trees had fallen into the valley, blocking whole areas and making the journey more arduous.

We had to scramble across slick boulders and walk across fallen trees. Such was the environment of the valley that it took hours to walk a distance one could have done in thirty minutes in England. Our progress was so slow we realized we would not make it to the end of the valley and back to camp before nightfall, and had to turn back about three quarters of the way along the valley. Darkness falls with alarming rapidity in the tropics. The river was treacherous enough by day, in the dark it would be deadly. A broken leg or even a sprained ankle in such a remote area could mean death, so we sadly turned back and headed towards the camp.

We decided that from where we were camped it would be impossible to reach the end of the valley in a day. Our small area was the only part of the valley suitable for camping, so we had no choice but to climb up the cliffs to the top again. In my opinion the lost valley did not look like suitable orang-pendek habitat. It was too narrow and there was nothing in it we discovered worthy of expending all the energy necessary for descending into, and I think orang-pendek would have more common sense than to needlessly climb down into such a gorge.

The climb back up was much easier than going down. We could crouch on all fours making ourselves more stable. Once we reached the top we found a new place to make a fresh camp, and Pak En took us off to where he had seen the orang-pendek. It was a long climb up through harsh jungle. Along the way we saw scrape marks left in the earth by a tiger, and it was odd to think we were sharing the forest with such large predators, a feeling one seldom gets in Britain. Some people we spoke to had lived their whole lives in the jungle and had never seen a tiger. Sahar had only ever seen one and Mr. Subandi had seen a total of three.

When we reached the area of the sighting Pak En mimed the strange way it was walking, gripping at the plants as it went. He told us its outsized muscles reminded him of the American heavyweight boxer Mike Tyson.

After returning from the jungle to what is laughingly called 'civilization' in Sumatra we headed for Banko, a town in Jambi province from whence we would enter the lowland jungles. Here we were to meet with the Suku Anak Dalam, the aborigines of Sumatra and interview them about the orang-pendek.

Sahar knew a man in Banko who spoke the language of the Suku

Anak Dalam and who could translate for us. We set out the next day together with our translator for a bumpy ride along an ill-maintained road leading into the jungle. The Suku Anak Dalam were once a totally nomadic tribe. Their only weapons were spears, foregoing even blowpipes or bows. They are far taller than the average Sumatran (who are of Malayan decent), with curlier hair. These days they are semi-nomadic, spending months in the jungle then returning to live for a while in houses.

We found a chief, a man named Nylam, in a roadside house with his family and several members of his tribe. He had been suffering from malaria and was glad when I was able to give him some medicine, and seemed happy to take us into his home and speak with us.

Chief Nylam while climbing a tree had witnessed an orang-pendek in the area only three months before. He said the animal was 1.25 meters tall and covered with red tinted, black hair. It had a broad mouth, walked upright and held its arms like a man. It made a WEEEEHP! WEEEEHP! noise and looked about itself as if it could smell its observer. Nylam said he watched it for half an hour.

Soon we had to return to England and it was to be five years before I returned to Sumatra.

Chris Clark joined me again and there were two new faces. Adam Davies was a fellow explorer and cryptozoologist. The year before I had been to Russia with him in search of the almasty, a relic hominid said to inhabit the Caucuses Mountains. He had visited Sumatra on several occasions before. Dave Archer was a CFZ member who had also been on the Russian trip and was keen to come with us to search for the short-man. (CFZ is the Centre for Fortean Zoology, the world's largest mystery animal investigation group, based in England but with offices globally.)

Adam contacted an Indonesian named Dally who was to act as a 'fixer' for us in Sumatra. Dally and Sahar met us at Padang airport where we were joined by John, Sahar's brother who we knew from previous expeditions, and another guide called Doni.

For the first part of the trip we planned to stay with the Suku Anak Dalam people Chris and I met in 2004. For the second half of the expedition we were to return to Gunung Tuju, the Lake of Seven Peaks, a jungle-swathed crater of an extinct volcano in Kerinci Seblat

National Park. There had been a number of orang-pendek sightings there in recent months including one by an ornithologist.

After a long journey we finally reached the rangers hut on the outskirts of town, where we were to apply for permits to stay in the lowland jungles. There are only around 2000 Suku Anak Dalam left so the Indonesian government are protective of them. Unfortunately, the head ranger was away in Java for two weeks and we could not get permits to stay, but we were permitted to visit the Suku Anak Dalam and speak with them.

We walked a couple of miles to a meeting point in the jungle where a small number of the Suku Anak Dalam were waiting for us. This group seemed shyer than those we had met in 2004. Women and children ran away and there was only one man with the group, the other men away hunting in the jungle. The man who seemed afflicted with scabies around his feet would not give us his name but still told his story through a translator.

Three years previously he had seen an orang-pendek close to the wonderfully named village of Anoolie Pie some 23km away. He said the creature was around 4 feet tall and covered with black hair. The creature's face reminded him of a macaque, with a flat nose and broad mouth. It stood and walked on two legs, never once dropping down on all fours. He insisted it was not a monkey, gibbon or sunbear, and the creature seemed afraid of him, walking quickly away whilst looking from side to side.

That evening we had a visit from an unassuming man called Tarib, supreme chief of the Suku Anak Dalam. Most of his people were away hunting but he had made a special effort to visit us and had an amazing story to tell.

Five years ago he had seen an orang-pendek as he was walking in the forest. It was four feet tall, with black hair that shaded into blonde and grey in places. Its face looked like a monkey's but it walked upright like a man. His path had taken the creature by surprise and it became aggressive, raising its arms above its head and charging him. He fled and hid behind a tangle of rattan vines, watching unobserved as it looked for him, turning its head from side to side before finally moving away.

This is one of the very few reports in which an orang-pendek was purported to act aggressively. In all other cases the creature has moved away quickly from the presence of humans, although there is a story that during the construction of the Trans-Sumatran Highway, machinery was attacked by groups of orang-pendek wielding sticks as weapons.

The next day we were up early for the long, hard climb up to the Lake of Seven Peaks. We crossed the lake again on the same, crumbling canoes that looked as if they would sink at any moment, then set up our camp. After breakfast we split into two teams in order to cover more ground. Adam, Dave, Sahar and Doni would take one track to a place where Adam had found and cast an orang-pendek track in 2001. Chris, John, Dally and I would take another track closer to the lake.

Dave brought four camera traps and Chris had a number of sticky boards. These are actually methods of pest control, cardboard strips coated with a powerful adhesive laid out to trap rats, mice and insects. We intended to place them on jungle paths baited with fruit, in the hope an orang-pendek would leave some of its hairs stuck in the solution.

Our trail led for several miles abreast of the lake where we came across some orang-pendek tracks. I had seen similar prints before and instantly recognized the narrow, human-like heel and the wider front part of the foot. The tracks were impressed in loam on the forest floor and not good enough to cast, but their very presence led us to set up two camera traps and two sticky boards baited with fruit, should the orang-pendek decide to return and grace us with some samples.

Upon returning to camp we heard amazing news. Whilst walking through the jungle, Adam, a mean tracker in his own right, heard a large animal moving through the forest. In the distance siamang gibbons were kicking up a fuss. Sahar and Dave crept forward and were greeted by a most amazing sight:

Squatted in a tree around 100 feet from them was an orang-pendek! They could not see the face clearly as it was pressed against the tree trunk. Dave felt it was peering at them from the side of its face. He saw the creature's eye rolling around in alarm and could see large teeth in the bottom jaw. The creature had broad shoulders, long powerful arms but the hands and feet were not in view. The orang-pendek had dark brown fur, almost black, the consistency reminding Dave of that of a mountain gorilla. This does makes sense as the jungles here are of a very similar type to those inhabited by mountain gorillas in Africa. The shape of the head recalled that of a gorilla as well, but the high forehead was more like that of an orang-utan. The head lacked the long mane of hair described by some witnesses, although he could see a line of darker hair running down the creature's spine. Dave approximated the orang-pandek to be the size of a large male chimpanzee, and he was adamantly sure it was not a sunbear nor a siamang gibbon.

Next to the tree was some rattan vine the animal had been chewing. Adam carefully placed this in a specimen tube full of ethanol in the hopes some of the cells from the creature's mouth would have adhered to the plant as they would to a cotton-tipped DNA swab. A number of hairs were also found close by and catalogued away for later analysis.

The next day we checked the camera traps and sticky boards. The former had captured nothing, the latter only insects, so we reset the camera traps and set out fresh sticky boards.

We did discover more tracks but our plaster of Paris had degraded in the humid conditions and was useless. We continued our camera setting and hiking for several more days with no results save for a picture of a small bird. That afternoon we decided to cross the lake and search on the far side. Adam had only been there once and the rest of us had never seen the area.

The guides strapped the three canoes together with rattan to construct a crude catamaran. The waters of the lake were calm so we made the 40-minute crossing without incident. We waded ashore to steep-sided jungle slopes that seemed far less disturbed than they had been on our side of the lake. The lack of adequate clearings to make camp meant even the local fishermen rarely visited this side of the water.

It was even damper on this side of the lake. Everything seemed spongy and had a rotten feel to it. We came upon a set of orang-pendek tracks clearer than any we had seen before, with the individual toes clearly visible. We photographed them extensively and cursed our lack of plaster to cast them.

On the crossing back the waters became quite choppy and rough and the canoes almost sank.

After a short rest we went and collected all of the camera traps and sticky boards. We returned to the tree where Sahar and Dave had seen the orang-pendek. We photographed the scene from the witness perspective, with our fixer Dally sitting in the same location as the creature. Under Dave's guidance we measured how large the upper part of the creature would have been from buttocks to the top of the head, with a result of three feet and four inches, making the animal — even if it had comparatively short legs—quite large.

After a long, long journey via Padang and then Singapore we arrived home. I sent half of the samples off to Lars Thomas at Copenhagen University. Adam sent his half to Dr. Todd Disotell of New York University. Lars studied the structure of the hair and found it was similar to but distinct from orang-utan. He commented that he was forced to conclude there was a large, unknown primate in Sumatra. His colleague Dr Tom Gilbert found some DNA in the sample that seemed to be human, which we believe resulted from contamination during collection. Conversely, Dr. Disotell could not extract any DNA from his sample.

Shortly after my return to England, Dally emailed me twice to tell me of further orang-pendek sightings in Kerinci. On October 8th some bird watchers from Siulak Mukai Village saw an orang-pendek near Gunung Tapanggang. They watched it for ten minutes from a distance of only ten meters. It had black skin, long arms and walked like a man.

On the 18th of October a man called Pak Udin saw an orang-pendek in Tandai Forest. The creature was looking for food in a dead tree, possibly insect larvae. It had black and silver hair, long arms and short legs. He watched it for three minutes before it ran away.

In 2011 I was back in Sumatra as part of an international team. Adam, Chris, Dave and I were joined by Andrew Sanderson, a veteran of a number of expeditions. Jon McGowen, naturalist and taxidermist, Tim de Frel, a Dutchman who worked for CITES (Convention on the International Trade in Endangered Species) and Australians Rebecca Lang and Mike Williams, who run the Australian office of the CFZ, rounded out the team.

The group was to split in two with Chris, Dave Andy and I taking the highland jungles, and Rebecca, Mike and Jon exploring the lowland jungles and the 'garden' area. Tim would alternate between the two groups.

Before we split up Sahar introduced us to a witness in his village. Pak Entis had seen an orang-pendek in April of that year within the garden area. He described it as three feet tall with massive shoulders and tan-coloured hair. It had an ape-like face and walked erect whilst swinging its arms. Upon noticing Pak Entis it became nervous and began to shake, raising its arms above its head and making a 'HOO-HOO' sound before moving away. It was in view for around 60 seconds.

Our team made the grueling climb up the slopes of the mountain and the uncomfortable crossing of the lake to our camp area. The next morning Sahar took us into the jungle. On the first day Sahar found and destroyed four snares set by poachers. It was the first time I had seen snares in the area and proved to demonstrate how human pressure is mounting in the park.

We set up our camera traps and discovered chewed rattan and fruit, as well as a rotten log that had been pulled apart. There were no claw marks such as a sun bear would leave.

The following day we moved to the far side of the lake where the ground is damper. Beside a rotting log overturned by some powerful animal Sahar found a handprint. The animal had braced itself with one hand whilst overturning the log with the other. It had apparently torn the log apart looking for grubs. Andy quickly took a cast using plaster of Paris, and nearby hair samples were found and taken.

The hand measured 6 inches long by 4.5 inches wide. It had a rounded palm and thick, sausage-like fingers. The thumb short and almost triangular. The print was nothing like the handprint of a Sumatran orang-utan, with its long thin fingers, palm and almost vestigial thumb. All in all it looked more like the handprint of a small gorilla in configuration. The shape suggested that its owner would have been able to manipulate objects and use tools.

The rest of our days yielded little more and the camera traps turned up nothing. We did however find the skeletons of two tapirs killed by tigers. Too soon we had to make the return trek home.

Late in 2012 I was contacted by a French filmmaker called Christophe Kilian. Chris had worked on a number of projects for Scienti Films, a French company that specialises in science documentaries. Chris wanted to make a film about 'wildmen' around the world but focusing mainly on orang-pendek. Chris had read my book 'Orang-pendek: Sumatra's Forgotten Ape,' and wanted to return to the jungles of Kerinci Sablat National Park with me to look for evidence of the creature.

The project was pencilled in for January, but was delayed until late June/early July, which, as it turned out, was a piece of serendipity. Joining us would be the beautiful and talented artist and taxidermist Adele Morse. I met Adele in 2011 when she contacted me wanting information on orang-pendek. Adele had found my writings about the creature online and had decided to do an installation or art project on the creature for the Royal Academy. I gave her as much information as I could, and sent her a copy of my book. She came up to Exeter for the weekend to interview me and subsequently made a number of life-size replicas of orang-pendek.

Sadly, our former guide Sahar passed away just a few weeks following our 2011 expedition. Dally, acting as a fixer had contacted Sahar's brother Jon and his Son Raffles to act as guides. At Polempek, Sahar's village, the fixers had gathered a group of witnesses for us to interview. It was to my knowledge the largest group of orang-pendek eyewitnesses ever assembled. All of the men were locals and had seen the creature or its tracks in the area within the last year. With the fixers translating, Adele and I interviewed whilst Chris filmed.

- Herman Dani had seen the creature Uhan Danda a year ago. He only got a good look at the head. The face had a flat nose and thin eyes. Its fur was grey. The creature stared at him and he ran away.

- Salim had seen strange tracks in the jungle five months before. He said they were man-like and the size of a human hand.

- Amri had his encounter at Padutingi, about four hours from Polempek, seven months previously. The creature he saw was one meter tall with grey fur. He ran away in fear.

- Juha Rapti had come across prints eight months before at Sungi Minya, around four-and-a-half hours away. They were human sized but had a highly separated big toe.

- Rahman saw the orang-pendek five months past at Gunung Sanka, about one hour away. The creature was large with black hair that faded to grey. It was moving quickly and he didn't get a good look at it. He fled.

- Saba Rudin saw the creature as it crossed a jungle trail. The area was between Sungi Mina and Sungi Kuni, about five hours away. The event happened ten months before. The orang-pendek had a broad, barrel-like chest and black and grey hair. It walked on two legs like a man.

- Aprisal was in the Sungi Kuni area nine months ago hunting wild pig. When he paused he saw a creature with black and grey fur and a large mouth. Afraid, he ran away. The area was about four hours distant.

- Mah Darpin saw the orang-pendek after rainfall at Gunnung Kacho, nine hours distant. He saw the creature from the back noting it had long fur of a grey-black colour, was around a meter tall and walked on two legs. He became afraid and walked back the way he had come.

- Saimi Alwi saw the creature one year before at Sungi Minya which is about four hours from Polempek. Whilst tracking he heard a noise and saw a creature squatting to eat kitan fruit. The animal was barrel-chested and muscular. It had black and grey fur and stood a meter tall.

All of their stories were remarkably consistent and I was struck by the lack of exaggeration.

The next day we began the arduous climb up the rim of the extinct volcano that forms Gunung Tuju. After resting at the top we descended to Gunung Tuju itself. I was horrified to see that the boulders at the edge of the lake had been defaced by graffiti. It seems true wilderness is getting harder and harder to find.

We made camp. Adele, Chris and I had our own tents whilst the guides and fixers erected a pondok, a large shelter made from branches, palm leaves and plastic sheeting. As the sun was setting and a fire was being started a primate call unlike any other I have heard rang out from the forest. I am familiar with all the calls of the wildlife in this area. I have also kept all the local primates in captivity. This was the call of a primate, but one I had never heard before. The vocalisation went 'ho...ho...ho...ho'. The guides and porters froze and John Dimus said 'orang-pendek'. Chris frantically tried to record the sound but it ended by the time he had his equipment ready and the call was not repeated.

It sounded relatively close to camp, and was no doubt an exciting and ominous start to the expedition.

In the morning we trekked into the jungle. There was much evidence of tiger activity nearby, within only a mile of the camp we found tiger claw marks on a tree trunk and came across two tiger kills. Both victims were Malayan tapir and the bones had been picked clean. Adele took a coccyx and vertebra as well as some teeth for her art display.

It was late June and a fruit called the kitan by locals was ripe and falling. About the size of a pineapple with a reddish-brown, hard outer skin and a yellowish pulp inside, it is said to be favoured by the orang-pendek. I have not yet been able to find the scientific or western name for this fruit. The guides said only the orang-pendek favours it. We found several that looked as if they had been chewed by something with human-like teeth. Close by John found a hair, but touched it with his fingers! We still preserved it in ethanol and set up a camera trap baited with fresh mango.

The following day we decided to explore the far side of the lake and set out in the rickety canoes. We climbed up a ridge and listened to screaming gibbons calling. Whilst the rest of us were listening to the gibbons Adele came across a track. It was on a slight slope, but it clearly showed the human-like heel and broader front foot typical of an orang-pendek.

I had brought some dental cement with me, a kind of fine plaster of Paris ideal for casting tracks. I tested the substance out in my garden back in Exeter to see how much was needed to make a cast, and to practice until I got the consistency correct. As the substance was heavy I carried only as much as I needed to cast a couple of tracks.

Adele offered to make the cast as she was a sculptress. However, I had not reckoned with the greater moisture in the rainforest and the more porous consistency of the ground. The casting of this single track took up all the dental cement I had brought.

Adele tried to strengthen the cast with strips of cloth, and once dry we gingerly eased it from the damp earth. It was not the best track I have ever seen, but the heel and toes were visible. The detail was somewhat blurred by the action of the bunching up of the earth around it on the slope. The cast cracked in two but Adele offered to take it back to London and repair it.

A few minutes later we came across two hand prints that looked very much like the one found by Andrew Sanderson on our 2011 expedition. I was gutted that I had run out of dental cement. On future expeditions I will know to take far more than I think I need.

The following day we followed another trail in the jungle in a different direction. Half-a-mile from the camp we came upon another orang-pendek track close to a rotting log. We also found and collected hair samples in the area. Whilst taking the samples we heard the call again. 'Ho…ho…ho…ho,' and yet again Chris was foiled in his attempt to record the vocalisation.

We moved further into the jungle and found another rotting log. Beside it was a set of the most perfect orang-pendek prints I have ever seen. No more than a day old, they were perfectly preserved in the damp soil. They clearly showed the long, man-like heel, four toes at the front and the offset big toe at the side. They would have made amazingly detailed casts. Once more I cursed not having brought more dental cement. I had to make do with filming and photographing them.

I believe there are two keys to finding orang-pendek in Kerinci Seblat. Firstly, to visit when the kitan fruit is ripe in late June/early July. Secondly, rotting logs. There have been a number of reports of orang-pendeks seen ripping rotting logs apart presumably to find grubs and insect larvae. We found the prints of at least three individuals around rotting logs.

In the same area we found many hair samples, far more than on any other expedition. I filled all my specimen jars and preserved the samples in ethanol. Again we heard the now familiar call 'ho…ho… ho…ho' but further away in the jungle depths. We found chewed kitan fruit in the area as well.

On the way back to camp we were confronted by a mass of vegetation, a labyrinth of branches made up of both dead trees and fallen trees that were still alive. It was a hard climb across, round and through the jungle maze. Adele did particularly well as she has poor depth perception due to her lack of certain eye muscles.

The following day we set out to collect the camera trap. On the way we found more tracks, but these were not so clear as the ones near the rotting log. At the camera trap area we noticed the mangoes had remained untouched. On our way back we faced a second vegetational labyrinth like the one from the day before.

Back in camp we looked at the shots from the camera trap. It showed nothing except us putting it up and taking it down, but I was not surprised. When testing the traps back in England we found they had to be left up for weeks on end before they captured anything at all.

Eventually we made the long crossing back over the lake and climbed down the side of the crater. The crossing and trek took most of the day. We saw monkeys and pig hunters as we reached the lower forests. At Polempek the cars were waiting to take us back to Sungi Penuh.

We met up with Dr. Achmad Yanuar of the National University of Java. A primatologist, Dr. Yanuar had worked with Debbie Martyr and Jeremy Holden during the Flora and Fauna International orang-pendek hunt in the 1990s.

Dr. Yanuar unfurled a map of Sumatra and showed us all of the places he had hunted for the orang-pendek. He investigated sightings and findings of tracks over most of Sumatra, except for the north. In all of his years searching he never saw the creature himself nor found any tracks, but he interviewed many witnesses. It seemed even twenty years ago reports of orang-pendek were much more widespread. Today they seem to be mostly confined to West Sumatra and Jambi. Though its range has shrunken vastly and swiftly the creature seems to be hanging on in these areas. We saw the tracks of at least three individual animals in one small corner of Kerinci Seblat National Park, an area that covers 13,791 square kilometers.

Whilst online at the hotel, Adele found a news item of extreme interest. Dr. Tom Gilbert, a geneticist from the University of Copenhagen, with whom we had worked before, had begun an exciting new project. Dr. Gilbert was looking into extracting DNA from the blood in the guts of leeches to find out what animals they had fed on. Dr. Gilbert and his team got twenty-five leeches from the Annamite Mountains of Vietnam and successfully extracted mammal DNA from twenty-one of them. Mammals identified included the striped rabbit (discovered in 1995), the serow, the Chinese ferret-badger, and the Turong Son muntjac (only discovered in 1998). The DNA can remain intact in the leech's gut for several months. He went on to say the technique could be used on creatures such as the thylacine and orang-pendek. We intend to work with Dr. Gilbert and his leech method on future expeditions.

The following day we travelled to Banko. We wanted to find some lowland forest to interview Dr Yanuar in. However, the lowland forests were so degraded it proved hard. Most had been chopped down to make way for palm plantations producing palm oil. We checked into a hotel and then went out to talk to one of the Suku Anak Dalam.

We drove from Banko to a small roadside village to meet a Suku Anak Dalam man called Pak Tumcuggung. Pak Tumcuggung had recently converted to Islam and lived in a house, eschewing the old, semi-nomadic ways of his people.

He told us via a translator about his encounter. About forty years before, he had been walking through a graveyard about a mile from the village of Batanlumbhi. At the time the area was heavily forested. Today the jungle has been cut down to make way for palm oil plantations. It was the rainy season and about five in the evening Pak Tumcuggung came upon some odd-looking tracks. Then he saw a man-like, grey-coloured figure rise up from behind one of the grave markers. At the time he thought it was a ghost and referred to it as orang-hutan or 'ghost man.'

The creature stood around three feet tall with long, grey hair, broad shoulders and a pot belly. The face looked very human with broad cheek bones. Pak said the creature looked more like an orang-utan than a siamang gibbon. The two stood and stated at each other until Pak turned and ran. He looked back and saw it still standing there, simply watching him.

At the time he thought what he had seen was a ghost, because he stumbled across it in a graveyard, and it seemed to combine animal and human features. Now he realises he saw some kind of animal that he feels is related to the orang-utan, but lives on the ground rather than in trees. He feels it still exists but not in the same area due to heavy deforestation. His brother saw an orang-pendek that same year, very much like the one Pak Tumcuggung described except it had black hair rather than grey. Additionally, in 2010 local people heard strange calls from an area of the forest that was clearly not a siamang. Pak believed it may have been an orang-pendek.

Each time I have returned to the jungles of Western Sumatra I have uncovered more evidence for the existence of the elusive orang-pendek. After the Tasmanian wolf, the orang-pendek is the cryptid I think is most likely to exist, but just what is it?

I have come across orang-pendek tracks on several occasions. The tracks were clearly non-human. The big toe was offset and placed about a quarter of the way down the side of the foot, a characteristic feature of an ape. Having said that the print was different from any known ape species. I have worked with gorillas, orang-utans, chimpanzees and gibbons, and have seen their tracks in all kinds of mediums including, mud, sand, snow and sawdust. The tracks we found on Sumatra were different. The heel was very human-like but the front of the foot was broader. There were four toes at the front and an offset big toe. The big toe seemed much less prehensile than those of other apes.

This shape of foot makes sense for an upright walking, ground dwelling ape. The man-like heel would be necessary for weight bearing. For an animal that spent less time climbing than other apes the less prehensile toe also makes sense.

In all the interviews I have conducted with eyewitnesses, what they describe sounds like an ape rather than a hominan. Long arms, massive shoulders, little neck, much body hair, short legs, these all add up to an ape.

We may ask why in a jungle full of trees orang-pendek is upright walking and ground dwelling. Debby Martyr postulated that the creature was a recent development having evolved in the wake of the eruption of the Toba super-volcano around 75,000 years ago, which would have stripped the island of its trees. However this does not explain why the Sumatran orang-utan survived. I feel the orang-pendek has its origins further back in time.

Male Sumatran orang-utans walk bipedally when they come to the forest floor. But up in the trees they will also walk erect along branches. Traditionally, bipedalism is thought to have developed on the plains of East Africa, when hominids first left the jungles to exploit new food sources around 5 million years ago. Standing erect, so the theory says, gave them a better view of potential predators. The vervet monkey (*Chlorocebus pygerythrus*), demonstrates this kind of behaviour, rearing up to look about it for danger. But now it seems bipedalism may have begun to evolve in the jungles.

During a year-long study of the Sumatran orang-utans of Gunung Leuser National Park, Paleoanthropologist Susannah Thorpe of the University of Birmingham spotted apes in the trees a total of 2,811 times, including numerous instances where they walked erect. In 75 percent of these cases they maintained balance with their hands, and over 90 percent of the time their legs were stiff, unlike the bent-knee, bent-hip shuffle of chimps and gorillas, which also occasionally stand upright in trees.

The apes stood erect mainly to reach for fruit whilst on fairly narrow branches. Thorp postulated the straight-legged posture helped them balance in the same way as a gymnast on a trampoline. Paleoanthropologist Bernard Wood of The George Washington University in Washington, D.C. commented on those findings:

"Most of us had assumed that the only place where it's sensible to be bipedal is on the ground. A handful of fossil species dating from five million to 28 million years old, mostly before chimpanzees split from hominins, showed signs of upright posture and bipedalism, but "the evidence has been pretty flakey,"

Wood thinks the findings put these fossils in a new light and they may have been true bipeds who evolved bipedalism to reach for fruit. As the jungles shrank they took up bipedal walking on the ground, whilst the gorillas and chimpanzees took up knuckle walking.

The fossils in question were of course African, but could something similar have occurred in the jungles of Asia, ultimately giving rise to a number of bipedal ape species?

Sunda was a large landmass that once incorporated Sumatra, Borneo, Java, the surrounding islands and the Malayan peninsula and connected them all to mainland Asia. As melting glaciers flooded the oceans 19,000 years ago sea levels rose and the huge landmass became cut into the islands we know today. I have already noted the two known orang-outans had already speciated by some 400,000. We do not know why this occurred but the more gracile Sumatran and the robust Bornean separated. The robust form populated the eastern island of Borneo and the gracile the western island of Sumatra. A larger form, *Pongo hooijeri*, the size of a modern gorilla, and presumably a ground dweller, existed further north in what is now mainland Asia. Closely related and known only from its teeth and jaws was the huge pongid *Gigantopithecus blacki*. This latter species has left fossils in India,

Vietnam and China, some dating as recently as 300,000 years ago. Due to the wide shape of the jawbone it has been postulated *Gigantopithecus* was a biped, with the neck placed directly under the skull. If this is correct and if the rest of the animal was built on the same scale, then *Gigantopithecus* would have stood approximately 10 feet tall. Some believe the creature is not extinct even today and survives in parts of India, Tibet, China, the Himalayas and elsewhere, and is known as the larger type of yeti.

All of the above, including modern orang-utans seem to have been descended from a genus of ancient apes known as *Sivapithecus*. The three known species are *Sivapithecus indicus*, *Sivapithecus sivalensis*, and *Sivapithecus parvada*. They flourished 12.5 to 8.5 million years ago and in life had bodies shaped like chimpanzees, but with heads more like that of modern orang-utans. Another genus *Lufengpithecus* arose around 10 million years ago with three known subspecies: *Lufengpithecus lufengensis*, *Lufengpithecus hudienensis* and *Lufengpithecus keiyuanensis*. These may have descended from an earlier form of *Sivapithecus*. Morphologically they seem to fall between *Sivapithecus* and modern orang-utans. It is one of these latter species that modern orangs seem to have evolved from.

I think that when the speciation of the modern orangs began they split into not two, but three species. The robust *P. Pygmaeus,* the more gracile and more upright *P.abelii*, and a third, smaller, terrestrial species we today know as orang-pendek, the elusive man-ape of Sumatra.

Sasquatch Kidnappings in North American Folklore

by Micah Hanks

Reports of kidnappings and mysterious, unsolved disappearances have left a rather unusual mark on the study of unexplained phenomenon over the last few years. Particularly in UFO circles, it has long been supposed—with special emphasis laid during the 1970s and 1980s—that one great and often frightening component to the broader UFO mystery involves people being carried away from the safety of their homes to be studied by UFO occupants. Fortunately, these individuals are returned shortly thereafter, often with only a partial memory of what transpired while in the apparent "alien" presences.

Arguably, if one were to presume certain members of the public have indeed been carried away by alien visitors from time to time, it would take little more in the minds of certain advocates to begin supposing that, on occasion, perhaps some "specimens" were kept indefinitely. Thus, one interpretation firmly planted in the minority, amidst a plethora of theories about missing person reports filed every year, might be that these individuals are victims of such a purported extraterrestrial collection program.

By around the middle 1990s, the atmosphere surrounding UFO abduction reports began to change. Though much of the alien abduction literature would, and still has maintained its popularity, clinical recognition and subsequent diagnosis of certain neurological conditions began to also suggest there might be more to some of the abduction claims than the kinds of hoaxes hardened skeptics had supposed previously. In his book 'The Demon-Haunted World,' the late astrophysicist and cosmologist Carl Sagan wrote of one such condition that, little-known though it was just two decades ago, is well-recognized in the present day:

> "A common, although insufficiently well-known, psychological syndrome rather like alien abduction is called sleep paralysis.

153

Many people experience it. It happens in that twilight world between being fully awake and fully asleep. For a few minutes, maybe longer, you're immobile and acutely anxious. You feel weight on your chest as if some being is sitting or lying there. Your heartbeat is quick, your breathing labored. You may experience auditory or visual hallucinations– of people, demons, ghosts, animals, or birds." [1]

Jerome Clark, the eminent Fortean researcher who, quite often, has taken a cautious stride when stepping over such hurdles as those presented by far-out claims like alien abduction, was more open minded than Sagan, but nonetheless careful in his discussion of a subject for which, as he notes here, little beyond the circumstantial can be offered as supporting data:

"As stories go, it is hard to beat tales of grotesque, gray-skinned humanoids who abduct people and do odd things to their bodies inside UFOs. This characterization of them is not intended to poke fun at such reports, some of which are genuinely puzzling, nor at the real trauma some "abductees" suffer. Abduction reports, like other high-strangeness narratives, make the most extraordinary sorts of claims in support of which they produce only circumstantial evidence. Such evidence, which never rises above the consistent-with-the-hypothesis variety, ranges from unaccounted-for marks on abductees' bodies to patterns in the data that appear explainable neither by chance nor by cultural contamination. Few knowledgeable investigators, whether ufologists or mental-health professionals, doubt that the abduction phenomenon is an enigma; neither would many argue that the evidence so far available is sufficient to do anything more than keep the question open." [2]

The question, though remaining open as Clark notes, is one that might carry deeper undertones. Thus, one reading this present soliloquy may wonder what all this has to do—if anything—with the creature known as *Sasquatch* or "Bigfoot."

Surprisingly, the subject of Sasquatch may have a lot to do with traditions that involve purported abductions by non-human entities.

---

1   Sagan, Carl. *The Demon Haunted World*. Ballantine Books, 1997.

2   Clark, Jerome. *Unexplained!* Visible Ink Press, 1998.

Within the folklore surrounding belief in the creature, particularly among North American Indians of the Pacific Northwest, abductions carried out by Sasquatches represent a motif that reappears with notable consistency. In addition to the stories of the kidnappings themselves, parallels can be found between such early legends and folklore, and some of the odd elements present in modern claims of alien abduction; namely, the prevalence of sexual themes that occur in relation to Sasquatches kidnapping humans as "mates," and the similar motifs surrounding "hybridization" programs that appear in UFO lore.

Such parallels, while perhaps not offered here as a literal explanation for the occasional baffling missing persons case that arises, nonetheless may bear fruit in helping unravel the nature of folkloric beliefs that emerge from perceived encounters with the unexplained. Here, while discussion of North American folklore is offered primarily in an attempt to examine recurrent cultural themes between such phenomena, it is our opinion some analysis of tangible claims of disappearances occurring in wilderness areas today may warrant further investigation in relation to the abduction motifs found within indigenous traditions.

A number of cultural variations appear in Native American folklore that reference wild people resembling Sasquatch. Such beings are often described as larger and more beast-like than humans. The website of the group Native Languages of the Americas, a small, nonprofit organization whose online presence is "dedicated to the survival of Native American languages," includes a short summary of Native American beliefs associated with Sasquatch, along with more than two dozen names for Bigfoot-like creatures used by various tribes. The website states, "In the Bigfoot myths of some tribes, Sasquatch and his relatives are generally shy and benign figures—they may take things that do not belong to them or even kidnap a human wife, but do not harm people and may even come to their aid."[3]

A 1924 *Seattle Times* article, written shortly after an incident involving a group of miners who claimed they were attacked by Sasquatch creatures near Mount Saint Helens, Washington, said the creatures were actually a lost tribe of large, hairy Indians called the *Seeahtiks*, whose existence, it was said, every Indian in the Northwest

3   "Native American Bigfoot Figures of Myth and Legend." http://www.native-languages.org/legends-bigfoot.htm

knew of. The Seeahtik clan purportedly made their home "in caves, in the heart of the wilderness on Vancouver Island and in the Olympic Range, in particular Mt. St. Helens," and were believed to be close to eight feet tall. As with other Native traditions about Sasquatches kidnapping human wives, it was said the Seeahtiks did this as well, in addition to the capture of infants:

> *In the past generations they stole many Indian women and Indian babies. They lived entirely in the mountain, coming down to the shores only when they wanted a change of diet. The Quinaults claim they generally came once a year to the Quinault River, about fall. The Clallams say they favored the river area near Brinnon on Hood Canal. After having their fill of fresh salmon, they stole dried salmon from the Indian women.* [4]

Among certain Native American traditions, Sasquatch is not generally regarded as a benevolent figure. In particular, legends among the Kucadikadi band of Paiute Indians near Mono Lake, California, tell of the *Pahi-zoho*, Sasquatches in Central Californian native traditions which inhabited the Sierra Nevada mountain range. In the local legends, the Paiute and Pahi-zoho traditionally avoided direct interaction, although it was believed children who wandered far enough from Paiute encampments might fall prey to the creatures, particularly succumbing to those bearing red hair (three varieties of Pahi-zoho in different coloration are said to exist: black, brown, and red haired, the latter of the three believed to be the most aggressive). Other traditions held beliefs that during times of famine, these creatures may resort to hunting humans for food.[5] This may be considered notable due to its similarity to legends associated with Lovelock Cave, a location in Nevada where excavations in 1912 revealed a number of mummified human bodies, some of which were supposedly large in stature. Paiute legends referred to this location in relation to legends about giants called the *Si-Te-Cah*, which were allegedly trapped and killed by the Paiutes when they burned a large fire at the mouth of the cave after the Si-Te-Cah entered.

In another of the Kucadikadi legends, a story is told of a young Paiute woman abducted by a Pahi-zoho when she strayed too close

---

4   "Clue to 'Gorilla Men' found, may be lost race of giants." *Seattle Times*. July 16, 1924.

5   Yosemite Mono Lake Paiute Native American History. https://yosemitemonolakepai-ute.wordpress.com/2007/11/30/paiute-encounters-with-bigfoot-like-creatures/

to the edge of a forest while picking berries. When others heard her frightened screams, her fellow tribesmen ran to aid her, but found that she had vanished from sight.

A search party was organized the following day, and as the group ascended the Sierras in their search, they came upon the frightened girl, who emerged from the forest in a hysterical state, screaming and making gestures back toward the forest. Upon her rescue, the story she told was strange indeed:

> She told the people that as she was picking berries along the meadow by the edge of the forest when a Big Foot or Pahi-zoho had come out behind a tree and grabbed her. He was big, reddish and hairy and she screamed and screamed. He had carried her off and she thought for sure he was going to eat her, but instead he took her into the bushes and forced himself on her. She said he stunk so bad, that it was making her sick and it was extremely painful, that he didn't talk but grunted all that time.[6]

Upon completion of the consummation, the young Paiute woman feared the creature would kill her. However, the creature clutched the woman close to its body instead, and fell asleep with her in its arms. Terrified, the woman lay beside the creature all night, unable to sleep due to the foul odor and loud snoring. Finally, as dawn approached, the creature's hold on the woman lessened enough that she leaped away and fled, continuing to run until she met the search party which had gone after her.

The strange affair would not end here, however. Some time after her strange affair with the Pahi-zoho, the young woman began to show signs of pregnancy:

> The people stayed clear of her except her friends and family. Nine months later she had a son, a big red-headed baby boy who was very hairy. The people were scared at first and some of the men wanted to kill him, but the girl's mother prevented them. Later the people accepted him into the group, for he was a good hunter and he had uncanny natural abilities of sight and smell and was very strong. He married and his children came out more normal looking, but every now and then one of his descendants comes out hairy and with red hair. Many of his descendants are now

---

6   Ibid.

scattered in many of the Paiute tribes in California and Nevada.[7]

This story is not unique, however. J.W. Burns, a government agent and teacher who famously chronicled legends of the Chehalis Indians and their encounters with the Sasquatch (a borrowed term, to which Burns is credited with the first use in print), told a similar story, as recounted here by researcher Ivan T. Sanderson:

> *Mr. J. W. Burns (now retired and living in San Francisco) who had devoted a lifetime to the study of this business, unearthed an old Amerindian woman from Port Douglas at the head of Harrison Lake who alleged, and brought some seconders to confirm, that she had been kidnapped by one of these creatures in the year 1871, kept by it for a year, but finally returned by it to her tribal homestead because she "aggravated it so much" (though, she said, it had treated her with every consideration). This old lady died in 1940 at the age of 86. When abducted she was 17 years old and was, she stated, forced to swim the Harrison River by the [creature] and then carried by him to a rock shelter where its aged parents dwelt. This account comes from Mr. Burns who had for years enjoyed the confidence of this retiring Amerind. It has been embellished in various ways by others to the effects that the girl had rosin plastered over her eyes by the creature; that she became pregnant by it; and that she subsequently gave birth to a half-breed that either was stillborn, died shortly after birth, or is still hidden by her people from the eyes of the white man. She never said any of these things to Mr. Burns but adhered to her straightforward story till her death.*[8]

The account presented here is unusual, particularly since it implies the woman coexisted with the creature somewhat willingly and for an extended period. Though likely apocryphal, it should be noted sources close to Burns in his later years similarly doubted that he took such stories to be literal in nature.

Of the stories about humans abducted by Sasquatches in the Pacific Northwestern wilderness that began to appear during the early twentieth century, not all were associated with Indian tribes; nor were they relegated to male Sasquatches kidnapping human women. One

---

7   Ibid.

8   Sanderson, Ivan T. *Abominable Snowmen: Legend Come to Life.* Chilton Book Company, 1961.

story which may rival in strangeness any of those reviewed here, was featured at the website of the late Bobbie Short (Bigfoot Encounters) in 2007, as told by a man named John Lewis. He shared a story he heard from his grandfather, which involved one of his co-workers in a railroad operation that vanished for a period of several days. The man was eventually found injured, badly frightened, and having apparently lost his wits and his clothing. What became of his wardrobe was another story entirely:

> Grandpa was working for Southern Pacific Railroad and building track in the northern California-Oregon border area in the early nineteen hundreds, I do not know the year; during this work project, he was dispatched to work on a line camp in the woods, they had a base camp that the work crew worked from, and each week the work crews would split in to two man teams that would work an area clearing logs and ground, and at the end of one week they would go back to the base camp to check in and replenish their supplies, and then set out after the weekend for another week in the woods.

During this time, one of the two-man teams came back to base camp with only one man, they were told that the other man had disappeared. The group at the base camp apparently gave a brief search to no avail.

The next week the crews went out in two man crews and continued the work on the railroad line clearing. Some weeks later, I am not sure how long this was as the camp moved north and the group of railroad workers came upon the missing man; he was naked and hysterical/crazed, and apparently died soon after he was found. He told of being abducted by a female ape that kept him in a large open pit. During the time he was in the pit the man told of being forced to have sexual contact with the ape many times and said that the ape kept him in the hole or pit by licking his hands and feet raw, so he was not able to escape from the pit. Apparently my grandfather saw this man's hands and feet, and said that they were completely raw.[9]

Lewis's mother and her siblings, having been taught in school that no apes existed in North America, chastised their father about this story, having deemed it impossible.

---

9   Lewis, John. "Strange Tale of Bigfoot." http://www.bigfootencounters.com/stories/n_california1900s.htm

Numerous other stories exist that resemble those examined here, but none perhaps have garnered such fame as the tale of Albert Ostman. Well known as it is, a brief summary shall suffice here: In 1924, Ostman had concluded a one year stint working with a logging operation, and decided to take a vacation to the wilderness near Toba Inlet, Western British Columbia, where he sought to recover a lost gold mine. He hired an Indian guide while in Lund, who would escort him to the mouth of the inlet by boat. The guide told Ostman about another man who had been a heavy drinker, who had apparently managed to fund his vice after visits into the mountains, where he had presumably managed to locate just such a mine. However, during one of his trips, the man vanished, and locals around Lund suspected a Sasquatch killed the man. Ostman, however, told his guide he did not believe in legends about "mountain giants."

Ostman made arrangements with the guide who would return for him at a predetermined time and location, and then headed up into the mountains. After several days of hiking, he set up camp near a small stream between two cypress trees growing by a rock wall. Here over the course of several subsequent nights Ostman began to notice his belongings had been tampered with while he slept. Hoping to catch the invader in the act (which Ostman believed to be a porcupine), Ostman wore his clothes while in his sleeping bag, and placed several belongings down in the bag with him to keep them out of reach, including his shoes and his rifle. Intending to remain awake all night until the animal appeared, Ostman nonetheless succumbed to sleep, and was awakened later by something large lifting him up and carrying him within his sleeping bag. He heard the heavy breathing and the thud of the animal's footsteps as it carried him for what seemed several hours, and finally upon being released, he observed four large, hairy humanoids gathered around him, which spoke to each other in a language Ostman did not recognize. Eventually they left Ostman, who remained trapped in the large canyon for several days with the creatures.

Ostman described them as a family, with an older male (the one that brought him there) and female, a young boy, and a young girl that appeared prepubescent. Ostman had been convinced the large male brought him there to be a mate for its daughter, and related a number of aspects about the creatures and their daily habits, in addition to descriptions of them. He remained in the canyon several days with the creatures, and while they never harmed him (he recounts even being given roots to eat by the younger male, although Ostman still had some food of his own within his sleeping bag), he was not permitted to leave. Upon attempting to do so, the creatures would move ahead of him, and place themselves between him and the entrance to the canyon.

Ostman noticed the two males, particularly the older one, observing him while he was dipping snuff. He had the idea that he might make the creatures sick by allowing them to have it, and rolling the can over to the younger male, it carried the prize over to its father, who consumed the can's entire contents. The creature became violently ill, and during the commotion, Ostman evaded the older female by firing a single shot with his rifle and escaped.

As to why he hadn't simply shot and killed the creatures, he noted that with a 30/30 and only six shells, he wasn't certain he would have been armed adequately enough to kill the large male. However, Ostman did describe having been prepared "to shoot my way out" if necessary, once he decided to leave. Regardless, Ostman conveys a sense of compassion for the creatures, having hoped to befriend the children in an effort to see if the younger ones might help him escape. He further noted the young girl was little enough that he might have brought her along with him:

> I am sure if I could get the old man out of the way I could easily have brought this girl out with me to civilization. But what good would that have been? I would have to keep her in a cage for public display. I don't think we have any right to force our way of life on other people, and I don't think they would like it. (The noise and racket in a modern city they would not like any more than I do.)[10]

Ostman's tale, if it is indeed to be accepted as truth, does not present a case where coupling or sexuality were explicit elements. At very least, we can discern that in Ostman's *opinion* this seemed likely, in that he believed the father intended him to be a suitor for the young female.

Up to this point the abduction narrative as it relates to American folklore about the Sasquatch does often present the kidnappings in a

---

10   Green, John. *Sasquatch: The Apes Among Us.* 1978, B.C. Canada: Hancock House

framework of sexuality and interbreeding. Some traditions, like those of the Paiute Indians we covered earlier, do indicate beliefs that the creatures might be cannibalistic, or at least opportunistic with their feeding habits. This theme was reflected somewhat in the tale of Muchalat Harry, an Indian man who claimed to have been kidnapped in 1928 under circumstances very similar to Ostman's situation four years earlier:

> One night, while wrapped in his blankets and clad only in his underwear, he was suddenly picked up by a huge male Bigfoot and carried off into the hills. He was not carried very far, probably a distance of about two or three miles, at the most. When daylight came he was able to see that he was in a sort of camp, under a high rock shelf and surrounded by some twenty Bigfoot. They were of all sexes and sizes. For some time, they stood around him and stared at him. The males to the front of the curious group, females behind them and young ones to the rear. Muchalat Harry was frightened at first and his fear grew to terror when he noticed, he said, the large number of bones lying around the campsite. When he saw these he was convinced that the Bigfeet were going to eat him.

The Bigfeet did not harm him in any way. Occasionally one came forward and touched him, as if feeling him, and when they discovered that his "skin" was loose — it was in fact his woolen underwear — several came forward and pulled at it gently.[11]

As with Ostman's beliefs about the reasons for his capture, one might suppose some of the implications of Muchalat Harry's experience—namely his observation of bones strewn about the campsite—had been colored somewhat by the observer's own interpretations.

With the exception of experiences like that of Muchalat Harry, the majority of the Sasquatch abductions that appear in American Indian legends deal with creatures kidnapping Indian women to have as "wives." This theme carries over into stories of those like Ostman and John Lewis, who tell of men being kidnapped for the purpose of inter-species coupling. This is significant for two reasons: the stories of kidnappings are not exclusive to one specific gender, nor are they

---

11   Byrne, Peter. *The Search for Bigfoot*. Acropolis Books, 1975.

relegated solely to American Indian legends. A final parallel that emerges, however, brings us back to the discussion of purported UFO kidnappings, which over the years have featured remarkably similar themes of abduction, and to a lesser degree, intercourse and sexual assaults that are commonplace throughout Sasquatch folklore.

Two notable cases involving such themes are that of Antonio Villas Boas, a Brazilian farmer who on October 15, 1957, claimed to have been taken aboard an unusual aircraft, stripped of his clothing, and made to have intercourse with an attractive, large-eyed woman that never spoke but grunted instead, and on one occasion bit Boas on the chin.[12] Another, occurring more than a decade later involved Shane Kurtz, a teenage girl who purportedly went missing from her bedroom for a period on the evening of May 2, 1968, only to reappear in her bed the following morning with mud on her bare feet. Afterward, her menstrual cycle became disrupted, along with the inclusion of strange, pink marks that appeared on her abdomen. During a hypnotic regression some years later, Kurtz allegedly recalled being in the presence of beings that made her undress and undergo a physical examination. Then one of the beings (a leader of some kind, wearing, of all things, a scarf) announced Kurtz would be bearing his child, after which he proceeded to undress and force himself upon her.[13]

The two incidents mentioned here are among those closest in similarity to the sorts of abductions and attempted coupling we see in Sasquatch legends. Whether or not some cultural conditions or themes exist that might offer an explanation for this similarity is unclear, and perhaps beyond the scope of the present discussion. It is our opinion this is at least worth noting here, due to the fact the apparent similarities are seldom observed in other related literature.

In recent years there have been circumstances where the Sasquatch abduction motif has reappeared, if not having undergone a sort of renaissance. California researcher and former police officer David Paulides has written a number of books on disappearances that have taken place in National Parks, with special emphasis on trends between the separate disappearances, as well as cases that seem to defy logical explanations. Paulides does not make explicit associations between these disappearances and alleged Bigfoot activity in his

---

12   Dean, Paul. *Sex and the Supernatural.* Vega, 2003.

13   Ibid.

written works, though some have argued this appears to be implied, and at times rather strongly. Further evidence for this may be found in Paulides' earlier work, which did focus heavily on the subject of Bigfoot. Additionally, Paulides is Executive Director of North America Bigfoot Search, a group aimed at seeking to provide scientific evidence for the existence of Sasquatch.

To date no data exists which presents physical proof, biological or otherwise, which has succeeded in convincing academic institutions that Sasquatch exists. Despite this, others have maintained that even in lieu of physical evidence, anecdotal data mostly collected over the last century strongly supports there being some physical basis for the reports. If such a species exists, or has ever existed, a wealth of this anecdotal information also supports interactions between these creatures and human beings, along with sexual themes that emerge, and which mirror themes found in similar but unrelated literature.

The abduction motif as outlined here plays an integral role in the Sasquatch literature. Thus, in conclusion, it is our view that perhaps this element within the broader body of information relating to Bigfoot research may in fact be among the most important, in our hope to understand this as a cultural phenomenon. At the very least, perhaps it would rank as a close second, behind the more obvious necessity for hard, physical proof that would help us determine whether Bigfoot does, without any further question, actually exist.

.

The Sound of Sasquatch

By Nick Redfern

Within the field of Bigfoot-seeking, there is perhaps no more emotive issue than that which ties the creature to the worlds of the supernatural and the paranormal. It's an area of the enigma that fascinates me and one which I focus a great deal of my time upon. And I don't apologize for looking into those areas so many arrogantly dismiss out of hand. Indeed, there can be no doubt for the vast majority of people in the research community, the "Bigfoot is paranormal" theory does nothing but raise blood pressure, anger levels and stress! In other words, the belief Bigfoot is just an unknown ape and nothing else most definitely holds sway in the field of cryptozoology.

Despite what the majority of the community says, none can deny there are reported cases of Bigfoot vanishing in a flash of light, of the creatures becoming invisible, and of them having the ability to affect the human mind – and not always in a good way. As I know all too well, such reports are written-off – by so many Bigfooters – as misidentification, fantasy, and hoaxes. What if there was another and very alternative explanation? One which allows for Bigfoot to be a flesh and blood animal, but an animal possessing bizarre, extraordinary powers. Is such a thing really feasible? Incredibly, *yes*, it just might be. And it all revolves around a still not entirely understood phenomenon called infrasound.

I have in my files many reports where eyewitnesses to Bigfoot have experienced nausea, dizziness, confusion, a feeling of lightheadedness, and even temporary paralysis. Now the "Bigfoot is an ape" crowd might put all of this down to the effects of sheer fear, and the pumping of massive amounts of adrenalin when faced with something monstrous and unknown. In some cases that may well be the case. There is, however, another possibility. All of which brings us to the matter of the aforementioned infrasound – which is a very low frequency sound and specifically lower than 20HZ, which is at the extreme range of human hearing.

Sound, UFOs, animals, and warfare

Before we get to the matter of Bigfoot it's important to note a number of animals – and widely varying animals – use infrasound as a means of communication, including elephants, whales, and giraffes. It's a form of communication that can be achieved, incredibly, at distances in excess of 100 miles. When infrasound is directed at people, however, the results can be *extremely* strange and downright terrifying. Unusual and unsettling physical sensations and weird hallucinations are not untypical. Indeed, sound has played a role in numerous supernatural encounters. Let's begin with UFOs.

Sightings of UFOs in the skies of our planet have been reported for decades – and perhaps for hundreds and maybe thousands of years. But what about the sound of a UFO? Interestingly, there are numerous accounts on-record where UFOs have reportedly emitted deep, resonating, humming noises that seem to exert some form of both physical and mental influence over the witnesses. Not only that, but such encounters have also left eyewitnesses feeling distinctly ill and disorientated.

The night of 20 August 1957 an Argentine guard was standing watch near a U.S. Air Force aircraft that had crashed near Quilino, Argentina. Suddenly, he heard a curious hum and was amazed to see above him a large, seemingly metallic, disc-shaped UFO. In stark terror, he attempted to draw his pistol, but with the humming sound becoming deeper and deeper, he found himself unable to do so and was certain his very self-will was under extreme threat. Most fascinating of all, the guard then had an overwhelming sensation that his mind was being overwhelmed by information from an intelligence aboard the UFO, information revolving around mankind's misuse of atomic energy – a topic he perceived was of great concern to those inside the craft.

Likewise, in December 1967, a woman was driving along Route 34 to Ithaca, New York, when she became aware of an unidentified red light that seemed to be following her. Glancing out of the window, she was shocked to see an illuminated object maneuvering near a row of power lines: "It made a humming sound, something like the vibration of a television antenna in the wind," she later stated.

As with the Argentinean Air Force guard, the woman reported

she felt the humming sound was taking away her self-will – and she also found her car would not respond properly. Interestingly, she added her son – who was in the car with her – "was in some kind of trance" during the time the UFO was in view.

But most notable of all is something that has become known as the *Taos Hum*. Throughout the late 1980s and 1990s, literally hundreds of residents of Taos, New Mexico, reported their lives had been adversely affected by a strange humming sound that proliferated throughout the entire area. And it may not be without relevance, in the same time frame a number of profound UFO encounters occurred in the vicinity. Speculation that the sounds were possibly the result of secret Department of Defense experiments led U.S. Representative Bill Richardson to initiate inquiries. Unfortunately he hit nothing but a brick wall.

Then there is the matter of what government agencies know of sound and how they may be using it against us...

Via the terms of the Freedom of Information Act, the Defense Intelligence Agency has released a remarkable series of files pertaining to classified experiments conducted to determine the effects of sound waves – particularly infrasound - on the human body. Most pertinent of all, one section of the files deals with certain effects of ultrasound on human beings – effects that can lead to drowsiness and an abnormal need for sleep:

"Another effect of ultrasound was disturbances in sleeping patterns. The need for sleep was felt by one group during actual work. Some individuals were overcome by drowsiness and in longer pauses fell asleep standing up, or in other, normally uncomfortable positions."

More alarming, the files state the U.S. Department of Defense was studying (as far back as 1972) research by the Soviets, who were trying to determine if both high- and low-frequency sound waves could be utilized to induce heart-attacks in otherwise healthy people.

As demonstrated in the above UFO witness accounts, sound has long been associated with the domain of UFOs, paranormal activity and even government secrets. Those cases cited above don't directly relate to infrasound, but I make use of them to specifically demonstrate that sound – in relation to strange phenomena – can have a drastic effect on the human mind and body. Now let's take a look at the world of the afterlife. We're talking ghosts and infrasound.

The matter of ghosts

"Mysteriously snuffed out candles, weird sensations and shivers down the spine may not be due to the presence of ghosts in haunted houses but to very low frequency sound that is inaudible to humans," said The Associated Press in September 2003, adding: "British scientists have shown in a controlled experiment that the extreme bass sound known as infrasound produces a range of bizarre effects in people including anxiety, extreme sorrow and chills — supporting popular suggestions of a link between infrasound and strange sensations."

"Normally you can't hear it," said Richard Lord, an acoustic scientist employed at the National Physical Laboratory in England who worked on the project.

"Some scientists have suggested that this level of sound may be present at some allegedly haunted sites and so cause people to have odd sensations that they attribute to a ghost - our findings support these ideas," added Professor Richard Wiseman, a psychologist working at the University of Hertfordshire in the U.K.

With all of the above described – demonstrating a clear link between matters of an unexplained kind and sound – let us see how the United States' most famous monster and infrasound go together, hand-in-glove.

Bigfoot disables those that search for it

Melissa Adair, an authority on Bigfoot states: "People who work with elephants have reported nausea, dizziness, vomiting, disorientation and weakness as a result of being exposed to the infrasound that elephants produce. The known effects of infrasound on humans include feelings of intense fear or awe. Bigfoot researchers have reported similar symptoms that seem to come on suddenly when out in the field. Are we being 'zapped'?"

Yes, quite possibly that is *precisely* what's going on.

Sasquatch expert Scott Carpenter noted on his personal encounter with one of the creatures:

"I am not an acoustic expert or a scientist. My findings are based on observation and common sense. I think that I was under the influence of infrasound during my encounter with the Bigfoot on April 30th, 2010. The Bigfoot manipulated my perception and sanitized my memory. Even more disturbing was the fact that I did not react to observing the Bigfoot. I had to have initially recognized what it was and where it was hiding. I made two attempts to zoom in on the Bigfoot and get a close-up video. Sometime during this process, I was subjected to the influence of infrasound and strongly influenced or 'brain washed' into walking off. It is almost like my memory was wiped clean and I was given instructions to leave and I did."

Similarly, "Miss Squatcher" has recorded the unsettling effects of her own encounter, at Elbow Falls, Alberta, Canada in the summer of 2013. She tells us: "I felt as if my chest was heavy, my breathing was shallow and I could hardly catch my breath. I stood up from examining the scat and scanned my surroundings, the sensation of my pulse pounding in my head. I saw nothing. I could feel panic setting in. I was on the edge of a full-blown panic attack and had the unrelenting feeling that I needed to leave the area, NOW. My anxiety was increasing and I shared this with the others. They were startled when I took out my compass, oriented myself in the direction we had come and started walking straight through the bush. 'I have to leave, I don't feel right.'"

She asked an important question: "Was there a Bigfoot nearby producing infrasonic waves to scare the heck out of us? We will never know for sure. But I can say with certainty that something out there made me feel more fear and panic than I have ever felt before."

It should be noted not every Bigfoot investigator is convinced Sasquatch uses infrasound to dissuade people from seeking it and pursuing it. One of those is Lisa Shiel, the author of such books as *Backyard Bigfoot* and *Forbidden Bigfoot*. She observes: "People who report feeling anxious or afraid when near a Bigfoot may simply be anxious and afraid because they are near a Bigfoot. I've seen plenty of strange things in my life, and often I feel anxious when those things happen. It's a natural human response. Must we attribute such responses to a poorly understood type of sound waves?"

It's a fair question, one upon which the Bigfoot-seeking community has no solid consensus. There can be no doubt, however, the effects people report are indeed indicative of infrasound. I know this, as I have experienced it myself. It was a memorable experience I could have done without.

A road trip and an unsettling experience

Texas' Ray Roberts Lake and its surrounding areas are notable and historical. In centuries long gone the lake was home to several Native American tribes, including the Comanche, Tonkawa and Kiowa. It was an area I visited one particular afternoon in early 2008 with Lance Oliver, who runs the Texas-based group, DAPS (the Denton Area Paranormal Society). Lance told me some months earlier there had been a number of interesting UFO encounters in the area. In May 1990, strange roaring and screaming noises of a distinctly animalistic nature were also heard in the woods. Notably, and at the very same time, an approximately eight-foot-tall, hair-covered man-beast was seen late at night by several young men camped out on the north side of the lake.

I followed Lance in my car as we drove to a small parking area, just about as close as a person could get by vehicle to where all of the specific Bigfoot action took place eighteen years earlier. We then made an approximately mile-long trek through the thick, surrounding woods, up and down several very steep climbs, and across a couple of rocky sandbars, against which the lake's cool waters gently lapped. Finally we got to the location where all of the hair-raising – and hairy – action had occurred. It was a wide and steep hill packed from floor to ceiling with dense trees and rotting vegetation. In addition there was a seeming lack of animal life and noise. "Deathly quiet" would be an understatement.

Even though the Bigfoot encounters occurred many years before, experience has shown me one should never turn up the opportunity to conduct a deep investigation of such a mysterious locale – just for the possibility something of profound interest might turn up. And it did turn up. In spectacular style.

Taking into consideration the heavily wooded hill was a very large one, Lance and I decided the wisest approach would be to split up and cover as much of the area as possible. In doing so, both of us stumbled upon what looked very much like the so-called "Bigfoot Teepees." These curious structures are essentially comprised of thick branches, that in many cases look like they have been wrenched off trees and placed into distinct pyramid-style formations. Some researchers have suggested they are made by Bigfoot creatures as territorial markers.

The reality, however, is we simply don't know enough about Bigfoot and its activities to make a solid determination on the reasoning behind their creation.

It was as Lance was exploring elsewhere I began to feel uneasy, clammy and short of breath. I should stress I have been on numerous expeditions in search of equally numerous unknown animals, and never experienced this feeling before. Nor am I someone of a nervous nature, and I'm not someone prone to panic attacks either. But in this occurrence it took all of my willpower, concentration and strength to try and control my breathing, to relax, and to banish from my mind the distinct feeling that unseen and hostile forms of a Bigfoot kind were doing their very best to force me out of the area. Albeit by using the power of infrasound, rather than muscle-power.

It was a very bizarre experience, one which I have never forgotten. Now let's take a look at one of the most controversial aspects of the Bigfoot phenomenon: the possibility they have the ability to render themselves invisible. As in *literally* invisible. You may well ask what that has to do with infrasound? Well, read on.

Invisibility and Bigfoot

Most investigators of the Bigfoot phenomenon take the view that the beasts they seek are flesh and blood animals that have been incredibly lucky in terms of skillfully avoiding us, or getting captured and killed. There is, however, another theory that may explain how and why Bigfoot always eludes us, at least when it comes to securing hard evidence of its existence. It's a theory that posits the creatures have the ability to become invisible – that's to say, they can "cloak" themselves so we do not see them. It's a theory that the bulk of Bigfoot enthusiasts have absolutely no time for. It is a fact, however, regardless of what people think of the theory, there is certainly no shortage of reports.

The website *Native Languages* notes: "The Bigfoot figure is common to the folklore of most Northwest Native American tribes. Native American Bigfoot legends usually describe the creatures as around 6-9 feet tall, very strong, hairy, uncivilized, and often foul-smelling, usually living in the woods and often foraging at night...In some Native stories, Bigfoot may have minor supernatural powers - the ability to turn invisible, for example - but they are always considered physical creatures of the forest, not spirits or ghosts."

Native Americans aren't the only people who hold such beliefs. *Bhutan Canada* says:

"In 2001, the Bhutanese Government created the Sakteng Wildlife Sanctuary, a 253 square-mile protected habitat for the Migoi. The sanctuary is also home to pandas, snow leopards, and tigers but the Bhutanese maintain that the refuge was created specifically for the Migoi. Migoi is the Tibetan word for 'wild man' or more common to Western culture, the Yeti. The Yeti, often called the Abominable Snowman in the west and referred to as the Migoi by the Bhutanese, is a bipedal ape-like creature said to inhabit the Himalayan region of Nepal, Tibet, and Bhutan. The Migoi is known for its phenomenal strength and magical powers, such as the ability to become invisible and to walk backwards to fool any trackers."

Davy Russell in 2000 penned an article titled *Invisible Bigfoot*, and therein refers to an incident that occurred in 1977, and which may be relevant to this particularly charged area of research. The location was North Dakota: "A Bigfoot-type creature was spotted throughout the afternoon and into the evening. Locals, along with the police, staked out the area to search for the mysterious creature. A rancher named Lyle Maxon reported a strange encounter, claiming he was walking in the dark when he plainly heard something nearby breathing heavily, as if from running."

Russell continued, stating that Maxon shone his flashlight in the direction of where the sounds were coming from but nothing could be seen. Puzzled and disturbed by the encounter, Maxon gave serious thought to the possibility the beast had the ability to render itself invisible to the human eye.

In April 2012, researcher Mai-Li said: "This past week, I had several wonderful conversations with a gentleman named Thomas Hughes. Thomas has been communicating with numerous Sasquatch since his first encounter in April 2008. He has a wealth of knowledge about their existence and whereabouts, some of which he shared with me.

"Sasquatch are gentle and playful giants. They range in height from 6-15 feet and live to an age of approximately 120-140 years. They are natural pranksters and are caretakers of Mother Earth. What I mean by caretakers is that they have adapted themselves to the planet instead of trying to change the environment to suit them…"

Mai-Li added that Hughes said: "They have the ability to raise their frequency just enough to be able to become invisible to humans. They fear humans – seeing them as their greatest threat. So, most of the time, they go invisible when humans are around to avoid being hunted and killed. Sasquatch are aware they are seen from time to time."

On a similar path, *Soul Guidance* offers that Bigfoot is "able to shift the frequency of their physical body, by which it phases out of this physical dimension, and thus enters another dimensional world that lies behind this one…

"Bigfoot can also shift partially, so they become invisible but are still partially in this physical world. In this partial state, they can follow someone around, invisibly, and their movements can be heard and seen. In this partial state, they can walk through walls; and they can sometimes be seen as being transparent, or just the outline of their body. For example, bushes move aside when they step through. When they appear or disappear, their eyes often turn red, probably a characteristic of the shifting frequencies…"

Infrasound and invisibility

Despite the body of evidence described above, there is another possible answer that may explain this very curious Bigfoot invisibility angle. Given the fact infrasound when directed at a person can cause major disabling effects, consider the following possibility as a working hypothesis: it may well be the creatures are not literally becoming invisible after all. That's not to say the witnesses are lying, however, as I don't believe they are.

What I *do* think is feasible is when a Bigfoot makes just about the biggest mistake possible, namely, being seen by a human, it attacks them with infrasound. Then when the person is in a distinctly altered state of mind, and their perceptions are deeply affected for what may be up to several minutes, the Bigfoot quickly exits the area and heads for the safety of the deeper woods. The result from the witness' perception, is the Bigfoot is there one second and gone the very next. The witness perceives this sudden – as in instantaneous – vanishing act to have been achieved by nothing less than the animal having rendered itself invisible. But if the person was under the mind-altering effects of infrasound at the time, the reality might be quite different.

I don't think it's at all impossible, nor unlikely that the mind-scrambled witness is unaware of what they *assumed* was an instantaneous vanishing, may actually have occurred over the course of twenty or thirty seconds, or even longer. In other words it only *looks* like the Bigfoot vanished in the blink of an eye. From the perspective of a bystander the picture might appear very different: a dazed and confused witness in a semi-trance-like state, stands rooted to the spot and not in full possession of their faculties, and the Bigfoot exits the area at high speed. In a few moments the witness returns to normal, but has a very different perspective than that same bystander on what actually happened. Or didn't happen.

A trip across the pond

During the course of undertaking research for a book dealing with landscape-based mysteries, one informant told Andy Roberts, a well-known English authority on paranormal phenomena, of a terrifying mountain-based experience that occurred to him during the early 1960s. The source was a boy at the time, and out with a friend to investigate one of the many aircraft wrecks from the Second World War, that still today litter the 2000-foot-high Bleaklow plateau in the Derbyshire Peak District of England. While visiting the crash site the man suddenly heard his friend shout, but the reason for his cry had nothing to do with the remains of old, wrecked aircraft.

The man told Roberts: "I looked and saw, all in one instant, grouse exploding out of the heather towards us, sheep and hares stampeding towards us and behind them, rolling at a rapid rate towards us from the direction of Hern Clough, a low bank of cloud or fog but what was truly terrifying was that in the leading edge of the cloud bank - in it and striding purposefully towards us - was a huge shadow-figure, a man-like silhouette, but far bigger than a man, as high as the cloud bank, as high as a house. And the terror that hit me and was driving the birds and the animals and my friend was utterly overwhelming - like a physical blow - and I have never felt the like since!"

"We fled," the man added, and continued thus to Roberts: "We plunged over the crags above Gathering Hill - and every time I go back and look at those crags, I wonder why we didn't break our necks. We fled in mindless terror down that mountainside towards the Shelf Brook and Doctors Gate - and all the sheep and wildlife that could run or fly went careering down with us in utter panic. And then, about half way down, we seemed to run out into the sunlight - and it was all over! All of the panic was gone. The sheep stopped, put their heads down, and started to graze. Everything returned at once to normal. But back up there, on Higher Shelf Stones, wisps of mist were still coiling round."

The particular entity in this case was clearly much larger than the average Bigfoot, and admittedly does have certain supernatural qualities attached to it. We do however see this sudden overwhelming sense of panic develop - a classic side-effect of targeted infrasound - and which in this case affected both people and animals, and which ended as quickly as it began. Just like with Bigfoot in the United States.

Now, it's time to see how Bigfoot's infrasound-based abilities may allow it to have advance knowledge of earthquake activity.

Animals and Earthquakes

The U.S. Government's U.S. Geological Survey (USGS) notes:

"The earliest reference we have to unusual animal behavior prior to a significant earthquake is from Greece in 373 BC. Rats, weasels, snakes, and centipedes reportedly left their homes and headed for safety several days before a destructive earthquake. Anecdotal evidence abounds of animals, fish, birds, reptiles, and insects exhibiting strange behavior anywhere from weeks to seconds before an earthquake. However, consistent and reliable behavior prior to seismic events, and a mechanism explaining how it could work, still eludes us. Most, but not all, scientists pursuing this mystery are in China or Japan."

The USGS - which has studied the matter of animal-based responses to earthquakes very deeply - adds:

"We can easily explain the cause of unusual animal behavior seconds before humans feel an earthquake. Very few humans notice the smaller P wave that travels the fastest from the earthquake source and arrives before the larger S wave. But many animals with more keen senses are able to feel the P wave seconds before the S wave arrives. As for sensing an impending earthquake days or weeks before it occurs, that's a different story.

"A once popular theory purported that there was a correlation between Lost Pet ads in the *San Jose Mercury News* and the dates of earthquakes in the San Francisco Bay area. A thorough statistical analysis of this theory, published in California Geology in 1988, concluded that there was no such correlation, however."

We also have the following from the USGS:

"Another paper published in a scientific journal in the U.S. on this subject by a respected scientist in 2000 is summarized here. The paper poses this question: Is it reasonable for a seismic-escape behavior pattern to evolve, and can such a genetic system be maintained in the face of selection pressures operating on the time scales of damaging seismic events? All animals instinctively respond to escape from predators and to preserve their lives. A wide variety of vertebrates already express 'early warning' behaviors that we understand for other types of events, so it's possible that a seismic-escape response could have evolved from this already-existing genetic pre-disposal. An instinctive response following a P-wave seconds before a larger S wave is not a "huge leap", so to speak, but what about other precursors that may occur days or weeks before an earthquake that we don't yet know about? If in fact there are precursors to a significant earthquake that we have yet to learn about (such as ground tilting, groundwater changes, electrical or magnetic field variations), indeed it's possible that some animals could sense these signals and connect the perception with an impending earthquake."

The USGS concludes: "However, much research still needs to be done on this subject. The author suggests establishing a baseline behavior pattern that can be compared with reactions of various environmental stimuli, and then testing various potential stimuli in the laboratory. Of course, the presence of these stimuli still needs to be researched with regard to precursory phenomena preceding an earthquake, for if these signals aren't present in the environment before an earthquake, a connection is irrelevant."

So, what does this have to do with Bigfoot? The answer is quite a lot!

Government knowledge of the Bigfoot-infrasound issue?

In October 2012, Becky Oskin, a senior writer for the LiveScience website, penned an article titled "How Earthquakes Make the Ground Go Boom." It began as follows: "As earthquake waves ripple through the Earth, the crust buckles, rumbles and roars - both audibly and at infrasonic frequencies, below the range of human hearing. A new study finds the Earth's surface acts like a speaker for low-frequency vibrations, transmitting an earthquake's infrasonic tumult into the air."

The article continues: "'This is really the first successful model for earthquake infrasound. It means that we can predict what we expect to see from earthquakes versus underground explosions, for example,' said study author Steve Arrowsmith, a researcher at Los Alamos National Laboratory in New Mexico."

Oskin added: "Researchers have debated the source of infrasound for decades, suggesting it comes from directly above the quake's source or from vibrations in nearby mountains."

All of which brings us to Bigfoot.

Dr. Chip Hardesty met with an employee of the aforementioned U.S. Geological Survey who in 2007 was involved in the study of seismic activity in the Three Sisters region of Oregon. According to Hardesty's source, at the very same time seismic activity was afoot, he encountered a massive, ten-foot-tall, red-haired Bigfoot crossing a stretch of road in the area. Despite having worked in the area for around two decades, the man had never previously had any kind of Bigfoot encounter at all. One has to wonder if the creature had detected the quake-driven infrasound and was fleeing the area, in the event the seismic activity might reach disastrous proportions.

Given this story has a government angle to it, one has to wonder if someone in officialdom has taken note of the infrasound controversy. Such a scenario may explain some of the strange accounts involving witnesses to Bigfoot who claim to have later been visited by representatives of the government and the military.

Conclusions

We may never know for certain if Bigfoot is a creature that uses infrasound to protect itself, to keep itself free of harm from the human race, or to manipulate the minds and nervous systems of those that intrude upon its territory. As we have seen time and again however, infrasound *is* a viable candidate to explain much of the high-strangeness attached to the Bigfoot controversy, such as the invisibility angle, the feelings of sudden and irrational panic, and the overwhelming need of witnesses to exit the areas in which Bigfoot are encountered as quickly as possible.

I'm encouraged by the fact that even though so many dismiss it, in the last few years more and more people have come around to the idea Bigfoot may utilize infrasound, primarily from a defensive – rather than offensive – perspective. This is encouraging as it suggests people are realizing there is far more to Bigfoot than meets the eye. It's my hope this welcome, open-minded approach will provoke further research into this issue of Bigfoot and infrasound. And if further work *is* undertaken maybe we'll actually have a few answers in our hands, rather than simply ever-growing numbers of reports piling up in filing cabinets and on websites, blogs, and thumb-drives.

Whether a flesh and blood animal or something much stranger, Sasquatch may very well be a creature for whom the nature of sound – and its many attendant mysteries – plays an integral role in its life and survival.

Bibliography

Giants of the Piney Woods, Lyle Blackburn

Downing, Roger. "Youths Report Attack By the 'Hawley Him.'" *Abilene Reporter* 07 July 1977. Print.

Holley, David. "The Cuthand Critter." Scary Sasquatch Stories (www.network54.com/Forum). 06 Nov. 2001. Web.

Jones, Mark and Teresa Ann Smith. "Has Bigfoot Moved To Texas?" *Fate* July 1979: 30-36. Print.

Marrs, Jim. "Fishy Man-Goat Terrifies Couples Parked at Lake Worth." *Fort Worth Star Telegram* 10 July 1969. Print.

Marrs, Jim. "Police, Residents Observe But Can't Identify 'Monster.'" *Fort Worth Star Telegram* 11 July 1969. Print.

Moore, Bill. "His Face Is Pushed In And His Ears 'Point.'" *El Paso Times* 20 Sep. 1975. Print.

Power, Irvin. "Boy Says For Real Sighting of Monster Renews Marion Legend." *Marshall News Messenger* 01 Sept 1965. Print.

Redfern, Nick. "Revisiting the Chambers Creek Monster." Cryptomundo (www.cryptomundo.com). 09 Sep. 2013. Web.

Rice, John. "Killer Creature Stalks Vidor Area." *Orange Leader* 20 June 1978. Print.

Riggs, Rob. *In the Big Thicket: On the Trail of the Wild Man: Exploring Nature's Mysterious Dimension.* New York: Paraview Press, 2001: 78-82, 89. Print.

Staff writer. "A Wild Boy Caught." *The Statesman* (Austin) 21 July 1875. Print.

Staff writer. "'Bigfoot' Terrorizes Kelly Area." *The San Antonio Light* 01 Sep. 1976. Print.

Staff writer. "Direct Has Critter Too." *The Paris News* (date unknown) 1965. Print.

Staff writer. "'Hairy Monster' Stomping Around." *Denton Record-Chronicle* 23 July 1963. Print.

Unknown. "Concerning the Longview, Texas, Reports." *Bigfoot Bulletin* 31 Oct. 1970: 3. Print.

Unknown. "Town Fed Up With Monster Hunters." *United Press International* 20 Sept. 1965. Print.

Woolheater, Craig. "Bigfoot in Texas?" Texas Bigfoot Research Center (www.texasbigfoot.com). Oct. 09, 2004. Web.

"Preserving Texas' Natural Heritage." LBJ School of Public Affairs Policy Research Project Report 31. 1978. Map.

Websites

Bigfoot Field Researchers Organization: http://www.bfro.net

Gulf Coast Bigfoot Research Organization: http://www.gcbro.com

John Green (Sasquatch) Database: http://www.sasquatchdatabase.com

North American Wood Ape Conservancy: http://woodape.org

Texas Almanac: http://texasalmanac.com

Big Man on the Reservation, David Weatherly

Green, John, The Sasquatch File, Cheam Publications, 1st Edition, (1973).

Iverson, Peter, Dine: A History of the Navajos. University of New Mexico Press, First Edition (2002).

Landry, Alysa, "Tracking Bigfoot" *Farmington Daily Times*. February 4, 2012.

Mathis, Brandon. "Bigfoot might lurk in nearby bush" *Durango Herald*. September 29, 2013.

Rife, Philip, Bigfoot Across America. *iUniverse*, 1st Edition (2000).

Yurth, Cindy. "Bigfoot's stomping grounds. There's more to Upper Fruitland than Northern Edge casino. *Navajo Times*, January 26, 2012.

Navajo Cops, Season One. NatGeo television (2012).

Websites

Bigfoot Field Researchers Organization (BFRO): http://bfro.net/

Cliff Barackman: http://cliffbarackman.com/

Phantoms and Monsters: http://www.phantomsandmonsters.com/

Sasquatch Kidnappings
in North American Folklore, Micah Hanks

Sagan, Carl. *The Demon Haunted World*. Ballantine Books, 1997.

Clark, Jerome. *Unexplained!* Visible Ink Press, 1998.

"Native American Bigfoot Figures of Myth and Legend." http://www. native-languages.org/legends-bigfoot.htm

"Clue to 'Gorilla Men' found, may be lost race of giants." *Seattle Times*. July 16, 1924.

Yosemite Mono Lake Paiute Native American History. https:// yosemitemonolakepaiute.wordpress.com/2007/11/30/paiute-encounters-with-bigfoot-like-creatures/

Sanderson, Ivan T. *Abominable Snowmen: Legend Come to Life*. Chilton Book Company, 1961.

Lewis, John. "Strange Tale of Bigfoot." http://www.bigfootencounters. com/stories/n_california1900s.htm

Green, John. *Sasquatch: The Apes Among Us*. 1978, B.C. Canada: Hancock House

Byrne, Peter. *The Search for Bigfoot*. Acropolis Books, 1975.

Dean, Paul. *Sex and the Supernatural*. Vega, 2003.

The Sound of Sasquatch, Nick Redfern

Adams, Ronald L. and Dr. R.A. Williams. "Biological Effects of Electromagnetic Radiation (Radiowaves and Microwaves), Eurasian Communist Countries. Defense Intelligence Agency. 1976.

Begich, Thomas. "Sourcing the Taos Hum." http://www.earthpulse. com/src/subcategory.asp?catid=2&subcatid=8. Undated.

Carpenter, Scott. "Bigfoot and Infrasound." http://bf-field-journal. blogspot.com/p/theory-bigfoot-cancreate-and-use.html. 2014.

"Folklore of Bhutan – Migoi, The Yeti." http://bhutancanada.org/

folklore-of-bhutan-migoi-the-yeti/. March 1, 2013.

Ford, Luke. "UFO Sightings in 1957." http://thecid.com/ufo/chrono/chrono/1957.htm. 2007.

Gordon, Stan. *Silent Invasion: The Pennsylvania UFO-Bigfoot Casebook*. Stan Gordon, 2010.

"Infrasound." http://www.birds.cornell.edu/brp/elephant/cyclotis/language/infrasound.html. 2015.

"Infrasound linked to spooky effects." http://www.nbcnews.com/id/3077192/ns/technology_and_science-science/t/infrasound-linked-spooky-effects/ September 7, 2003.

Mai-Li. "The Habits and Whereabouts of the 'Sasquatch' aka 'Bigfoot.'" http://consciouslifenews.com/habits-whereabouts-sasquatch-aka-bigfoot/1126683/. April 5, 2012.

Miss Squatcher. "The Infrasonic Effects of Bigfoots." http://misssquatcher.blogspot.com/2013/10/the-infrasonic-effects-of-bigfoots.html. October 10, 2014.

"Native American Bigfoot Figures of Myth and Legend." http://www.native-languages.org/legends-bigfoot.htm. 2015.

Oskin, Becky. "How Earthquakes Make the Ground Go Boom." http://www.livescience.com/24209-earthquakes-infrasound.html. October 23, 2012.

Pritchett, Jeffery. "Melissa Adair Shares Her Bigfoot Encounter on Video." http://beforeitsnews.com/paranormal/2014/12/melissa-adair-shares-her-bigfoot-encounter-on-video-2479896.html. December 1, 2014.

Roberts, Andy. "The Big Grey Man of Ben Macdhui and Other Mountain Panics." Strangely

Strange but Oddly Normal. Woolsery, U.K.: CFZ Press, 2010.

Russell, Davy. "Invisible Bigfoot." http://www.bigfootencounters.com/articles/invisible.htm. February 29, 2000.

Shiel, Lisa. "Bigfoot Infrasound: Likely or Long Shot?" http://lisashiel.jacobsvillebooks.com/blog/bigfoot-infrasound-likely-or-long-shot/ March 7, 2014.

Soul Guidance. "Who is Sasquatch/Bigfoot?" http://www.soul-guidance.com/houseofthesun/bigfoot.html. Undated.

"Three Sisters, Deschutes County, Oregon April 2007." http://www.
bigfootencounters.com/stories/deschutescntyOR.htm. Undated.

U.S. Geological Survey. "Animals and Earthquake Prediction." http://
earthquake.usgs.gov/learn/topics/animal_eqs.php. September 29,
2014.

List of Contributors

Lyle Blackburn

Lyle Blackburn is an author, musician and cryptid researcher from Texas. His investigative cryptozoology books, *The Beast of Boggy Creek* and *Lizard Man* reflect his lifelong fascination with legends and sighting reports of real-life 'monsters.' During his research Lyle has often explored the remote reaches of the southern U.S., in search of shadowy creatures said to inhabit the dense backwoods and swamplands.

Lyle has been heard on numerous radio programs including Coast To Coast AM, and has appeared on various television shows airing on Animal Planet, Destination America, A&E, and CBS. Most recently, Lyle served as a consulting producer and special episode host for the tv show *Monsters and Mysteries in America*.

For more information, visit www.lyleblackburn.com

Credit: Claire Thomas, ABC News AU

Richard Freeman

Richard Freeman is a cryptozoologist, author, zoological journalist, WebTV Presenter, and zoological director of the Centre for Fortean Zoology (CFZ). Freeman has written, co-written, or edited a number of books, and has contributed widely to both Fortean and zoological magazines, as well as other newspapers and periodicals, including *Fortean Times* and *Paranormal Magazine*.

He has lectured across the UK at the Fortean Times Unconvention, the Weird Weekend, Microcon, the Natural History Museum, the Grant Museum of Zoology, Queen Mary, University of London and the Last Tuesday Society. All on pursuit of the Tasmanian wolf, orang-pendek, Mongolian deathworm, yeti, giant anaconda, almasty, ninki-nanka, Scottish and English lake monsters.

Richard credits an early obsession with the classic science fiction series Doctor Who (with Jon Pertwee) as sparking an interest in all things weird. After school, he became a zoo keeper at Twycross Zoo in Leicestershire and became head keeper of reptiles, working with more than 400 exotic species from ants to elephants (but with a special interest in crocodilians). After leaving the zoo, he worked in an exotic pet shop, a reptile rescue centre, and as a gravedigger.

Whilst on holiday he learned of the CFZ and bought a copy of the Centre's journal, *Animals & Men*, which left him impressed enough to subscribe and begin contributing. He eventually became the CFZ's Yorkshire representative, then moved to Devon to become a full-time member of the Centre. He is now the zoological director and co-editor of *Animals & Men* and the annual CFZ yearbook.

Ken Gerhard

Ken Gerhard is a widely recognized cryptozoologist, author and fixture on numerous paranormal TV shows.

He has traveled the world searching for evidence of mysterious beasts including Bigfoot, The Loch Ness Monster, the Chupacabra, flying creatures and even werewolves.

Ken has written several books and articles on the subject and his research has been featured on numerous TV shows including Monster Quest, Ancient Aliens and Unexplained Files. He has appeared on major networks including – CBS, Travel Channel, National Geographic, Animal Planet, Syfy, Science Channel and Destination America.

Currently, he is co-host of the History Channel series – Missing in Alaska.

Linda S. Godfrey

Author and investigator Linda S. Godfrey writes books about strange creatures, places, people and things from her home on the southern edge of the Kettle Moraine State Forest, Southern Unit. She is a frequent guest on national TV and radio shows such as Monsterquest, Lost Tapes, Monsters and Mysteries, Coast to Coast AM, Whitley Strieber's Dreamland, Wisconsin Public Radio and Art Bell's Midnight in the Desert. See a list of her books, blog and more at http://lindagodfrey.com

Micah Hanks

Micah Hanks is a writer, podcaster, and researcher whose interests cover a variety of subjects. His areas of focus include history, science, philosophy, current events, cultural studies, technology, unexplained phenomena and ways the future of human-kind may be influenced by science and innovation in the coming decades. He lives in the Appalachian Mountains near Asheville, North Carolina, and in addition to writing, podcasting, and research, Micah enjoys traveling and maintains a passion for science fiction, fine art, music from around the world, and the pursuit of all things unique and interesting.

You can follow Micah and his work at his website, www.micahhanks.com, and listen to his weekly podcast, The Gralien Report, at www.gralienreport.com.

Credit: Jon Downes, Fortean Zoology Blogspot

Richard Muirhead

Richard was born in Hong Kong in 1966, and his career as a cryptozoologist began in April 1977, when at the age of ten he read in Hong Kong's *South China Morning Post* about the carcass of a sea creature dredged up by the Japanese trawler *Zuiyo-maru* off the coast of New Zealand. Circa 1985, just after his father retired, he discovered he wasn't alone in his interest in the world of anomalous phenomenon. He came across *Fortean Times* and was immediately hooked.

In 1987 he attended the International Society of Cryptozoology Conference in Edinburgh, discussing the Loch Ness Monster. In 1994 he re-connected with Jon Downes, president of the Centre for Fortean Zoology U.K., a childhood friend from Hong Kong. He wrote for Downes' `Animals and Men` and continues the collaboration on an ongoing project called `The Mystery Animals of Hong Kong.`

In December 1998 British Wildlife magazine published his first article on peculiar zoology titled `Black Squirrels in Britain`. In April 2011 he launched issue 1 of `Flying Snake` which reached issue number 10 in March 2016. His concentration he dubs "archival cryptozoology," i.e. pre-1950 and covers the whole range of mystery animals, http://www.cosmicpolymath.com/blog/new-issue-of-flying-snake4. Richard has also been published in the *The Anomalist, The Cryptozoology Review, BioFortean Notes, The Centre for Fortean Zoology Yearbook*, and *The Amateur Naturalist*.

Nick Redfern

Nick Redfern is the author of 36 books on UFOs, lake-monsters, the Roswell UFO crash, zombies and Hollywood scandal, including *Men in Black; Chupacabra Road Trip; The Bigfoot Book;* and *Close Encounters of the Fatal Kind.* Nick has appeared on many TV shows, including: Fox News; the BBC's Out of This World; the SyFy Channel's Proof Positive; the History Channel's Monster Quest, America's Book of Secrets, Ancient Aliens and UFO Hunters; the National Geographic Channel's Paranatural; and MSNBC's Countdown with Keith Olbermann.

He can be contacted at: http://nickredfernfortean.blogspot. com

David Weatherly

David Weatherly has spent his life exploring the world of the strange, investigating the supernatural and paranormal around the world. He has written and lectured on a diverse range of topics including Cryptozoology, Ufology, Hauntings, psychic phenomena and ancient mysteries. David has also studied Shamanic traditions with elders from numerous cultures including Europe, Tibet, Native America, and Africa.

He is a frequent guest on both radio and television and is the author of several books including *The Black Eyed Children* and *Strange Intruders*.

For more information, visit: http://twocrowsparanormal.blogspot.com/

About the Editor
A. Dale Triplett

Arbra Dale Triplett is an author, journalist, copywriter, veteran and editor. He's been writing fiction, advertising, marketing and UFO-related content for more than a decade. Born in Springfield, Missouri to an Air Force family, he grew up in Texas, Colorado and Illinois before spending thirteen years in Germany. He studied English and History at Oklahoma Christian University, Harding University and Lubbock Christian. He served abroad in the Marine Corps for 4 years, drove semi trucks from coast to coast hauling anything from live bees to oversized freight, and flew in the Air Force as Loadmaster on a C-130 cargo transport. He's hung his hat from Alaska to Florida. You'll find him every year at the UFO Congress in Arizona, soaking up conversation at the fire pit with a cold beverage at hand.

Dale is the author of illustrated children's book *Benjamin Oliver Flanagan* and Science-Fiction/Fantasy *The Halcyon's Wake Chronicles*. Visit his website www.DaleTriplett.com and follow him on Twitter @DaleTriplett.

Printed in Great Britain
by Amazon